HOW W
GOVERNED

ELEVENTH EDITION

HOW WE ARE GOVERNED

ELEVENTH EDITION

FEDERAL
STATE AND
LOCAL
GOVERNMENT

CLAUDE R FORELL

Longman Cheshire

Longman Cheshire Pty Limited
Longman House
Kings Gardens
95 Coventry Street
Melbourne 3205 Australia

Offices in Sydney, Brisbane, Adelaide and Perth, and associated companies throughout the world.

Designed by Mary Kerr
Produced by Longman Cheshire Pty Ltd
Printed in Australia

National Library of Australia
Cataloguing-in-Publication data

Forell, C.R. (Claude Rainer), 1931–   .
   How we are governed.

   11th ed.
   Includes index.
   ISBN 0 582 80243 1

   1. Australian. Constitution. 2. Australia - Politics and government. 3. Australia - Constitutional law. I. Title

354.94

The
publisher's
policy is to use
**paper manufactured
from sustainable forests**

CONTENTS

PREFACE

How we are governed celebrates its thirtieth anniversary in 1994. This is the eleventh edition. It is significantly different from the first, although the basic structure remains. In 1964 Sir Robert Menzies still ruled in Canberra, and political life was less complex and more predictable. In its successive revisions, *How we are governed* has kept up with events and now even looks to the future, in examining the republican debate into which Australians are being increasingly drawn.

The book was originally suggested by Dr Andrew Fabinyi, of F.W. Cheshire, and one of his assistants, David New, a former colleague of mine at *The Age*. For more than fifty years, Cheshire had published *The Australian Citizen*, originally written by Professor Walter Murdoch, and later revised by a master at Scotch College, Melbourne. It had been widely used in civics courses in secondary schools, but Cheshire was eager for something more up to date and more directly focused on the Australian political system. As a young political science and history graduate with recent experience as a political reporter in Canberra and state political correspondent in Victoria, I was asked to write a new book with a contemporary approach.

In the early 1960s there were only three or four general books on Australian government and politics, aimed mainly at university students and concentrating on the Federal system. *How we are governed* was intended to offer an introduction to Australian government—Federal, State and local—in simpler language for students, immigrants and general readers, and to put it into a historical context. Perhaps that is why it has survived, despite the plethora of other books and official publications on Australian government and politics published over the past thirty years.

Claude Forell

WHAT IS GOVERNMENT?

Few of us realise just how much government is part of our everyday life. When you walk down the street to buy an ice-cream, you can do so reasonably freely and safely because government, through its armed forces, alliances with friendly nations and membership of international organisations, is ready to defend our country from possible enemies, and because government, through the law and the police, is there to protect you from being set upon, or robbed, or run over. Government has built the street you are walking along and coined the money in your pocket. It sets out where and when the shop may open for business, inspects the premises to see they are clean, and even tries to ensure that the ice-cream is pure and wholesome.

Some people think that there is too much government, too many politicians or that they have to pay too much in taxes. But no sensible person would say that we could do without government at all. A game of cricket or football would be impossible without rules, and without an umpire to apply the rules and settle disagreements. Life in a civilised community is far more complicated than a game. All who can afford it must help to pay for it. More rules are needed, and a stronger force is necessary to ensure that they are obeyed. If everyone could do just as they pleased—perhaps steal or cheat or kill—few of us would be safe and only the strong would survive. This is true for nations as for individuals.

THE TASKS OF GOVERNMENT

The purpose of government is to provide a system of order in which people can live. Government does not exist for its own sake, but to help us achieve what we want from life. It does this in a number of ways.

The first major task of government is to ensure the *security* of the country, by defending it against those who might attack it from without and against those who might try to overthrow the government from within by violence or treachery. The second task of government is to maintain *order*, by preventing members of the community from harming one another or disturbing the peace. Closely linked with this is government's third task; that of providing *justice* through the law courts and tribunals, where the law is interpreted and applied fairly and impartially in particular cases, and where disputes may be settled.

Even if everybody lived peacefully and lawfully, there would still be need for government. Many things necessary for the welfare of the community as a whole can be provided only by government, or done better by government than by private individuals or business—the building of roads and schools and reservoirs, for example, or the carriage of letters, or the prevention of the spread of disease. Thus the fourth task of government is to provide *public works* and *essential services*.

These four have been the traditional tasks of government for many centuries. But in the past eighty or ninety years, three more have become increasingly important. These days, government has largely taken over the job of helping the poor, sick and needy, in ways such as paying pensions to the elderly, disabled, widowed and deserted, and those who cannot find work. This fifth task of government is called *social welfare*. Government's sixth and increasingly important task is concerned with *economic policy*. Australians enjoy a relatively high standard of living, and look to government to preserve it, such as through measures to control inflation, protect jobs, promote trade and help market our farm and other products. The seventh task is that of *conservation and development*. This includes conserving our natural resources such as water, soil and forests, encouraging the search for oil and other minerals, engaging in scientific research that will help our agriculture and industry, protecting our wildlife and native plants, and preventing pollution.

FORMS OF GOVERNMENT

At the dawn of history, when people began to live in tribes or clans, government was fairly simple. It was entrusted to a chief, or a council of wise elders. As human society became bigger and more complex, so did government. The ancient Greek thinkers divided government into three forms: *monarchy*, or rule by one (usually a king); *oligarchy*, or rule by the few (the rich or noble or powerful); and *democracy*, or rule by the many (the free citizens). Each of these forms of government, when it overrode the rights or ignored the well-being of the governed, could turn into *tyranny*. In modern times, we have seen tyranny in the form of *dictatorship*, when one man or a party seized power, as in Nazi Germany under Hitler or Fascist Italy under Mussolini.

If one of the old Greek philosophers were alive today he would find it hard to classify the government of Australia. As we still share a Queen with Britain and her other realms, Australia could be called a monarchy. But because the laws are made, as we shall see, by a small group of people in Parliament, it would seem we are ruled by an oligarchy. Yet we pride ourselves on being members of a democracy, which Abraham Lincoln, in his famous Gettysburg address in 1863, described as 'government of the people, by the people and for the people'. The explanation is that government has changed a great deal over the centuries.

Although the Queen (represented in Australia by a Governor-General and six State Governors) is head of State, she is not an absolute monarch. Her representatives must govern with the consent of Parliament and according to the law. In other words, the monarch alone cannot make laws or disregard the laws already made. We have, therefore, what is known as *constitutional monarchy*. (In practice, it is not the Queen but her Ministers who govern, but we shall explain that more fully later.) Some countries, such as France and Italy, were once monarchies but have replaced their kings with elected presidents, thus becoming *republics*. The United States has been a republic since the Declaration of Independence on 4 July 1776. Australia might also decide in due course to become a republic.

PARLIAMENTARY DEMOCRACY

Most modern constitutional monarchies and republics are also democracies, though not exactly in the sense in which the Greeks used the word. Ancient Greece was not a single nation but was made up of a number of small states, such as Athens and Sparta. In these city states, every free citizen could take part in the government and was expected to do so. This is not possible in a country with millions of people. Instead, the people elect representatives who meet together in a parliament. This is known as *parliamentary democracy* or *representative government*. In Australia, as in Britain, representative government has been taken a step further. Not only are the elected representatives responsible to the people who chose them, but the Ministers who govern in the name of the Queen are chosen from and are responsible to the elected representatives in Parliament. This is *responsible government*, which we will look at more closely later. Australia, then, is both a constitutional monarchy (which might become a republic) and a parliamentary democracy. Each term draws attention to a different aspect of our Government.

All forms of government have one thing in common: they have authority—the power to make laws and compel people to obey them. But in a democracy this authority is based on the consent of the people, who can change the government by a majority vote in free elections. Democracy is possible only where the minority of citizens is willing to accept the rule of the majority, and the majority is prepared to respect the rights of the community. These conditions do not exist in many countries today.

SEPARATION OF POWERS

Government is the business of making laws, carrying them out, and deciding if they have been broken in particular cases. These functions are called legislative, executive and judicial. In a primitive society, or in a dictatorship, they may all be controlled by one powerful individual, group or party. But in a modern democracy, these three powers are usually in the hands of different and distinct bodies. The law-making body, or *legislature*, we call Parliament. The *executive* is the Government, formally headed in Australia by the Governor-General representing the Queen but actually led by the Prime Minister. The Government controls the public service, which carries out the day-to-day work of administration. The third body is the *judiciary*, as the system of law courts is called.

Although the Queen's Ministers are chosen from Parliament, they can normally govern only so long as they have the support of the majority of members of the lower House of Parliament. Although the judges of the law courts are appointed by the Government, they cannot be dismissed except by Parliament for the most serious reasons. This means that the judges are utterly independent, and can perform their duty 'freely and fairly, without favour and without fear'.

THE RULE OF LAW

The independence of the judiciary is part of our British heritage of government: another is the rule of law. No one may be arrested by the police unless suspected for having broken the law, or kept in prison unless a magistrate or judge and jury have found them guilty. No one may have their property taken from them by the government without legal authority and then only if compensation is paid. No one may be denied justice, for the law applies equally to the high and the mighty and the low and the humble. King John agreed to these fundamental rights in the Magna Carta in 1215, and they have become firmly woven into the fabric of the law that we have inherited and extended.

EQUALITY AND LIBERTY

Two other principles are basic to democracy as we know it—those of equality and liberty. By equality we do not mean that all persons are alike, but that each human being has an equal right to 'life, liberty and the pursuit of happiness'. Reformers were more successful in achieving legal equality than political equality—the idea that every citizen should have an equal right to vote in the election of Parliament. It took many years of struggle and reform before every adult man and woman, regardless of income and education, was given a vote. More recently, many people have become concerned with economic equality, the belief that there should not be such huge differences in wealth and opportunity between the very rich and the very poor. Our Government does something to even out these differences by imposing higher taxes on people with higher incomes, and by providing social security for the needy. A major difference between Australia's two main political parties is their attitude to how far the Government should go in ensuring a fairer distribution of the nation's wealth.

Just as equality does not mean that all people are exactly alike, liberty does not mean that a person can do exactly as he or she pleases. If car owners were 'free' to drive on the wrong side of the road, they would endanger the safety and freedom of other drivers (and themselves) to drive at all. The freedom of an individual must always be limited to the extent that it does not interfere with the freedom and well-being of others. Just law and good government, by restraining people from doing wrong, ensure their freedom to do what they believe to be right. Freedom of religion enables us to worship according to our conscience. Some freedoms are essential to the working of democracy. The right to vote is worth little unless a citizen is free to listen to and talk about facts and ideas, and read and write about them in books, journals and newspapers, and attend meetings and join organisations. Freedom of speech, freedom of the press and freedom of association within the law are among our cherished political liberties.

For further thought

- Democracy means different things to different people and nations. What do you understand by the term?
- Is parliamentary democracy the best possible form of government? Before you answer this, consider what you expect government to do, and how well our form of government does these things.
- Is democracy possible, or even desirable, in the newly independent nations of Africa and Asia, where democratic forms and values have not been able to evolve over many years?
- Absolute freedom is impossible in a civilised community. Where should governments draw the line between liberty and restraint?

CHAPTER

2

GOVERNMENT IN AUSTRALIA

The postal officer delivering your mail, the police officer patrolling the street and the neighbourhood garbage collector are all carrying out some of the familiar day-to-day work of government. Their duties differ, of course, but they are also a reminder that Australia has *three levels* of government—Federal, State and local. The post office is one of the services of the Federal Government. Post a letter to Darwin or Devonport, Brisbane or Broome, and it will cost the same postage and be handled and delivered by the same Australia-wide government organisation—Australia Post. The police force is an organ of the State Government. Officers can arrest criminals and direct traffic only within their own State; whereas the garbage collector is employed by the local council and works only within the municipal area.

This division of government into Federal, State and local means that most Australians are governed by three sets of laws and deal with three sets of officials—voters elect representatives to three sets of governing bodies. A typical Australian citizen living, let us say, in Bendigo, Victoria, would vote for members of the Federal Parliament in Canberra, Victorian State Parliament in Melbourne, and for members of the Bendigo City Council.

To understand why Australia should have a Federal Government, six State Governments and some hundreds of local government authorities, we must look into our history. Until 1901, Australia was a country and a continent, but not yet a nation. It comprised six separate British colonies. The first, New South Wales, was established by Governor Phillip as a convict settlement in 1788. Tasmania was separated from New South Wales in 1825 and Victoria in 1851. Western Australia was established as a separate colony in 1829, South Australia in 1836 and Queensland in

1859. Over the years, each gained a larger measure of self-government from Britain, and each developed its own parliament and laws and administration. (There are now also two territories within Australia—the Northern Territory and the Australian Capital Territory—which are largely self-governing under the control of the Federal Government.)

Each of the six colonial governments was made responsible for the whole range of government activities, other than such matters as defence and foreign policy, which were safely kept in the hands of the British Government. Drawing on British tradition and experience, the colonies decided quite early that local works and services—such as road repairs, street lighting and garbage collection—could be best organised by bodies of public-spirited persons in each town or district. So each colony was mapped out into municipalities and shires, in which the property owners were given the right to elect a council to decide what works were necessary, to levy rates to pay for them and to employ people to carry them out.

FEDERATION

Towards the end of the nineteenth century, the feeling grew among a number of Australians that some of the affairs of government that affected Australia as a whole should be conducted by a central government rather than by the colonial governments individually. The need for a united voice on defending Australia, freedom of trade among the colonies, and a common policy on immigration spurred on the movement towards Federation. Many people, too, were stirred by the idea of nationhood, and began to see themselves as Australians and not merely as Victorians or inhabitants of New South Wales.

The six colonies, if they wished, could have handed over all their powers to a new national government, to govern the whole country. But they chose to keep a measure of independence, and to give to the central government only those powers which it needed to deal with 'matters of common concern'. In short, they chose a federal rather than a unitary system of government.

The colonial statesmen who met at a series of conferences and national conventions to plan Federation decided to follow the American example of setting out the matters for which the Federal Government was to be made solely or jointly responsible. Everything else, including control of local government, was to be left to the States, as the colonies were to be called. As in Canada, the provincial governments kept certain limited powers and the rest were given to the Federal Government.

THE CONSTITUTION

The document drawn up to describe the structure of Federal Government and to list its powers is known as the Commonwealth Constitution. It was put together at a Second National Convention of elected and appointed colonial delegates who met at three sessions in Adelaide, Sydney and Melbourne in 1897–98. They reconsidered and built upon an earlier draft that was adopted by the First National Convention in 1891 but not readily accepted by the colonial Parliaments. New Zealand took part in the 1891 convention but decided to remain independent.

Before Federation and the new Constitution could come into effect they had to be approved by the Australian people and passed as an Act of the Imperial Parliament in London. Referendums in Victoria, South Australia and Tasmania in 1898 were passed by big majorities, but the majority in favour in New South Wales was less than that required by the NSW Parliament. After agreement was reached at a premiers' conference to make some minor changes, a second round of referendums in 1899 in these four colonies and Queensland approved Federation with bigger majorities. Western Australia unsuccessfully held out for further concessions until after the Constitution Act was passed by the Imperial Parliament in 1900. But it voted in favour of Federation in time to become a founding member when the Commonwealth of Australia came into being on 1 January 1901. The first Federal Parliament was opened in Melbourne on 9 May 1901.

Most of the matters on which Federal Parliament may make laws are listed in Section 51 of the Constitution. The most important Federal powers are defence, foreign affairs, control of trade and commerce, taxation (particularly customs and excise duties), pensions, immigration and postal services. Some of these powers are exclusive to the Commonwealth—no State may have its own army, mint its own coins, impose customs duties, or send ambassadors to foreign countries. Other powers, which are shared with the States, are said to be *concurrent*.

The States remained responsible for many things that affect our lives most directly—schools, hospitals, roads, railways, electricity and water supply, for example, as well as maintenance of law and order. If a Federal and a State law happen to conflict where legislative powers are concurrent, the Federal law overrules the out-of-step State law. This seldom occurs. Usually, where the Commonwealth and the States have concurrent powers they cooperate or look after different aspects of the work. In public health, for instance, the Commonwealth is responsible for quarantine—keeping dangerous diseases out of Australia—and the States are responsible for controlling infectious diseases within Australia.

In most countries, the constitution sets out the basic rules of the system of government, as well as the basic rights of the citizen. Some features of the Australian Constitution worth noting are:

1 It is essentially a compact between the Commonwealth and States, not between government and people. It sets out the structure and powers of Federal Parliament and Government, but has little to say about democratic and civil rights.

2 Many important aspects of our system of government are assumed or implied rather than expressly stated. These are left to *conventions*, the unwritten rules on which parliamentary government is based in Britain. For instance, the Constitution vests the executive power of government in the Governor-General as the Queen's representative. The Governor-General may appoint advisory Ministers and administer Government departments. However, in most cases a Cabinet of Ministers is chosen by and from the political party or coalition with a majority of seats in the lower House of Parliament. Cabinet, headed by the Prime Minister, not the Governor-General, is the real executive. Cabinet government and majority rule rely on conventions, not the Constitution.

3 The division of powers between the Commonwealth and States has also led to conflicts. Federal Governments do not have all the powers they may feel they need to govern effectively. State Governments are apt to complain that the Federal Government's superior tax-raising powers leaves them at a financial disadvantage and encourages the Federal Government to encroach on their rights and responsibilities.

4 Critics of the Constitution argue that it is too inflexible, restrictive, anomalous and conservative, forcing the political process to work within a framework that is too unresponsive to the needs of an advanced and changing society. Its defenders see it as a safeguard against over-powerful or radical government.

5 The Constitution is very difficult to change. Direct amendments generally require the people's consent by referendum, and the necessary political consensus under the complex referendum provisions is not easily reached.

6 Its wording is not always clear. This gives rise to uncertainty, disputes over its meaning and challenges to the validity of some Federal legislation. These disputes and challenges may be settled by the High Court, whose interpretation of the Constitution can change it quite significantly.

The Constitution and Federal–State relations are discussed in more detail in Chapter 9.

For further thought

- Would Australia be better off with a unitary system of government—a strong central government delegating some of its powers to regional councils—instead of the Federal system?
- Should the Commonwealth be given more powers, or should the powers and rights of the States be preserved and strengthened? Give your reasons.
- Should more States be created? If so, why and where?

3

PARLIAMENT

The British system of parliamentary government, on which our own is modelled, has evolved over many centuries. The Kings of England were never absolute monarchs, able to rule as they pleased. In feudal times, the King was bound to consult his barons on matters of great importance, and he summoned them to a 'parliament'. The word *parliament* comes from the French *parler*, to talk, French having been the language of the Norman conquerors. Edward I in 1295 began the practice of summoning representatives of the 'commons'—knights from the shires and burgesses from the boroughs (towns)—to the more important of these parliaments.

Soon the Lords and Commons began to meet separately in private assemblies to discuss their answers to be given to the King in Parliament. The Commons elected a Speaker to act as their spokesman to the King. Before long, when the Commons wanted a change in the law, they would submit to the King a petition or *Bill*. From the reign of Henry V (1413–22), the Bill was in the form the Commons wished the new law to be made. It was sent to the Lords for their agreement, and when it was approved by both *Houses*, the Bill was brought before the King in Parliament for royal assent. The Bill then became an Act of Parliament and part of the law of the land.

The British Parliament still consists formally of the Sovereign (King or Queen), the House of Lords and the House of Commons. Legislative sovereignty—the supreme law-making authority—is vested in all three together, and new laws are said to be made by the 'Queen in Parliament'. But as the power of the Sovereign diminished over the centuries, the meetings of the King in Parliament became more and more formal, and the real work of Parliament came to be done in the two Houses sitting

A model of the old Parliament House, Canberra, in the foreground and the new building, opened in 1988, on Capital Hill behind.

separately. Nowadays, the Queen actually sits in the British Parliament only once a year, for the formal opening of proceedings.

Parliament is thus a place in which laws are made and altered. Another important function of Parliament is to authorise the raising and spending of money for the needs of government. The principle that the people could not be made to pay taxes without the consent of Parliament was finally established in the seventeenth century after a long struggle between the Sovereign and the House of Commons. As a result, the King had to call Parliament to meet at least once a year to grant the funds needed for the expenses of government.

It is worth remembering three great struggles in the history of Parliament. The first ended with the Revolution of 1688, when the Houses of Parliament won supremacy over the King. The Bill of Rights of 1689 limited the power of the King for all time. The second struggle was to make the House of Commons democratic—truly representative of the whole people instead of only a small group of rich and powerful persons. The turning point in this struggle was the Reform Act of 1832, but it took almost a hundred years before every man and woman was entitled to vote. The third great contest, which has been substantially settled this century, was to ensure that the will of the elected House of Commons should prevail over that of the mainly hereditary House of Lords.

The Queen, Governor-General and Governors

Australia has seven sovereign Parliaments: Federal Parliament in Canberra and a Parliament in each of the six States. Formally each Parliament, with one exception, consists of the Queen and two Houses. The exception is Queensland, which now has only one House. The lower House of the Federal Parliament, modelled on the House of Commons, is the House of Representatives, and the upper House is the Senate. The lower Houses of New South Wales, Victoria and Western Australia, and Queensland's single House, are called Legislative Assemblies, while the lower Houses of South Australia and Tasmania are called Houses of Assembly. The State upper Houses are all known as Legislative Councils.

The Northern Territory, which might become the seventh State, and the Australian Capital Territory now also have Legislative Assemblies, but these have more limited powers than State Parliaments. Both territories have substantial self-government, but some matters remain under direct Commonwealth control.

Queen Elizabeth II is Queen of Australia as she is Queen of Great Britain and other members of the Commonwealth of Nations that recognise her as Sovereign. The Queen herself has very few real powers, and is represented in Australia by the Governor-General in Canberra and by a Governor in each State. They normally exercise all the formal responsibilities, perform the ceremonial duties and retain the discretionary powers that the Queen would carry out or hold in reserve in Britain, without any instructions or interference. Note that the Governors are not subordinate to the Governor-General; each is a direct representative of the Queen in his or her State. The Northern Territory has an Administrator responsible to the Federal Government. The term *Administrator* is also used for someone, usually a senior State Governor, standing in for the Governor-General during a temporary absence.

The time might soon come when Australians will be asked to vote on whether they wish their nation to become a republic and appoint or elect a president as Head of State, as many other Commonwealth countries have done. The arguments for and against such a change, and what it would mean, are discussed in Chapter 10.

The Queen, with the Duke of Edinburgh and the Prime Minister, Mr Bob Hawke, at the opening of Australia's new Parliament House on 9 May 1988.

The Governor-General is appointed by the Queen on the advice of her Australian Ministers, and it is now accepted that he or she should be an eminent Australian. In the past twenty-five years there have been five Governors-General: two former senior Federal politicians (Sir Paul Hasluck and Mr Bill Hayden), two former judges (Sir John Kerr and Sir Ninian Stephen), and a former university vice-chancellor (Sir Zelman Cowen).

The powers and duties of the Governor-General are laid down in the Constitution or established by custom. They include the formal power to summon and prorogue (end sessions of) Parliament; dissolve the House of Representatives before an election and in certain circumstances both Houses; fix times for the holding of parliamentary sessions; recommend bills for appropriation of money to the Parliament; assent or withhold assent to legislation; appoint and dismiss Ministers; and submit referendum proposals to the people. At the beginning of each session of Parliament, the Governor-General outlines the Government's programme of legislation in an opening speech. He or she also presides over the Executive Council, and is formally head of the armed services.

Constitutionally, the Governor-General exercises the supreme executive power of the Commonwealth Government as the Queen's representative. In fact, the Governor-General normally acts on the advice of Ministers, who are responsible to Parliament. As we shall see in the next chapter, the real heads of Government are the Prime Minister and the Cabinet. However, the Governor-General does have some discretionary or reserve powers. The Governor-General should be satisfied that an advised action is lawful. A request for the dissolution of Parliament, for example, must be justified. In some circumstances, the Governor-General may independently choose the Prime Minister. By convention, the Governor-General has three rights enjoyed by the Queen in England—to warn, to advise and to be consulted by Ministers. It has also been long accepted that the position should be politically neutral and impartial, and avoid public controversy.

Some of these assumptions were shaken in November 1975 when the Governor-General, Sir John Kerr, abruptly dismissed the Prime Minister, Mr Gough Whitlam, and his Government; appointed the Opposition Leader, Mr Malcolm Fraser, as head of a caretaker administration; and dissolved both Houses of Parliament for an election. It was the first time in any country with a British-style system of government that a Prime Minister, without warning and against his will, had been dismissed from office, not because he lacked majority support in the lower House but because he had failed to obtain supply (approval for government spending) in the upper House.

There is little doubt that the Governor-General has the legal power to dismiss a Prime Minister, but whether it was right and proper for Sir John Kerr to act as he did in the circumstances remains a matter of bitter dispute. In fairness to him, it may be said he faced a situation which had not happened before and which could not arise in Britain, where the House of Lords no longer has the power to withhold supply. The crisis has had three consequences:

1 most Australians realised that the Governor-General is more powerful than they suspected;
2 Sir John Kerr, his powers and his office became the subjects of intense controversy, which made it difficult for him to symbolise national unity;
3 as Sir John Kerr acted on his own initiative and as the Queen declined to intervene, it became clear that the Governor-General is not subject to the Queen's instructions or supervision in the exercise of powers.

Until 1986 State Governors were formally appointed by the Queen on the advice of her Secretary of State for Foreign and Commonwealth Affairs and formally represented the British Government as well as the Queen personally. But in practice, Governors had already been chosen by the State Governments, and Britain no longer directs them or involves itself in the government of its former colonies. The duties and powers of the Governors are similar to those of the Governor-General, and some have not hesitated to exercise their discretionary powers. Governors have refused a dissolution of Parliament and one dismissed a Premier who had a majority in the New South Wales Legislative Assembly (on the grounds that he had contravened a Federal law).

In the past, distinguished Britons were usually chosen for the position of Governor-General or Governor, but now the pattern is to appoint Australians. South Australia appointed both the first Aboriginal Governor, Sir Doug Nicholls, in 1976, and the first female Governor, Dame Roma Mitchell, in 1991. When the Governor-General is temporarily absent, a senior State Governor acts as Administrator in his or her place.

THE STATE PARLIAMENTS

Parliamentary government began in Australia in the colonies, as the States were called before Federation. When Governor Phillip established New South Wales, he was empowered 'to make ordinances for the good government of the settlement'. Although he was responsible to the British Government for the way in which he ruled, his powers within the colony were almost those of an absolute monarch, and his orders had the force of law. In 1823, the Governor was given a small council to help him make and carry out laws, but its members were nominated by the Governor and not elected by the colonists.

It was not until 1842 that New South Wales gained representative government. A Legislative Council was established, with two-thirds of its thirty-six members elected and one-third nominated. But the executive part of government—carrying out the laws—was still in the hands of the Governor and his officials. In 1850 Britain gave New South Wales, Victoria (formerly part of New South Wales), South Australia and Tasmania substantial self-government. This was extended to Queensland in 1859 and Western Australia in 1890.

Self-government opened the way to responsible government. Within a few years, the colonies had drawn up their own constitutions, providing for two Houses of Parliament and for Ministers to be chosen from, and responsible to, freely elected local parliaments. The Legislative Councils became the upper House, and the new lower Houses were named Legislative Assemblies or Houses of Assembly. Later, Queensland and Western Australia followed the same pattern when they were given self-government.

Note that it is in the lower House of each Australian Parliament that Governments are made and unmade. As we shall see in the next chapter, the Government is formed from the party or parties with a majority of members in the lower House.

THE LOWER HOUSES

Despite Australia's unpromising beginning as a convict settlement ruled by despotic Governors, the struggle for democracy was more quickly won than it was in Britain. The colonists elected to the early Legislative Assemblies and Houses of Assembly did not regard government as being largely the preserve of a privileged class, as in England. Many of them were rough-and-ready men, who saw government as a means of developing their new country and of ensuring that everyone shared in the benefits. They wanted cheap land for settlement, roads and railways, and later, protection for the new industries, better working conditions and social services. To help achieve these aims, they fought to establish democracy.

Within a few years of responsible government, the lower Houses of most of the Australian colonies were elected by universal manhood suffrage: every man, regardless of his property, income, education or station in life, was entitled to vote in an election. And to prevent electors from being intimidated, the vote was by secret ballot. Elections were to be held more often than in England (usually every three years instead of five), electoral districts were made reasonably equal, and working men were not prevented from standing for Parliament by having to be property owners. Later, Australia was also among the first countries in the world to give the vote to women, and to pay salaries, allowances and pensions to members of Parliament.

NUMBER OF MEMBERS OF PARLIAMENT, JULY 1993									
	Federal	NSW	Vic	Qld	SA	WA	Tas	NT	ACT	Total
Upper House	76	45	44	-	22	34	19	-	-	240
Lower House	147	99	81	89	47	57	35	25	17	597
Total	223	144	125	89	69	91	54	25	17	837

THE UPPER HOUSES

The men who framed the colonial Constitutions, being more conservative than those soon to be elected to the new lower Houses, did not want to see democracy unchecked. They felt it prudent to safeguard the rights of property, and believed that men of property, wealth and education had more of a 'stake in the country' than the gold diggers, city workers, smaller townsfolk and farm labourers. So they made sure that legislation considered to be too radical could be blocked in the upper Houses—the Legislative Councils.

This they did by ensuring that the Legislative Councils were not elected by all the people. In Britain, the House of Lords remained conservative because it was composed mostly of hereditary peers. In Victoria, South Australia, Western Australia and Tasmania, the right to vote was restricted to people with property or certain other qualifications. In New South Wales and Queensland, members of the early Councils were nominated by Government. From 1934 to 1978, New South Wales Legislative Councillors were chosen by members of both Houses voting as an electoral college.

There were many bitter struggles between the democratically elected lower Houses and the restricted upper Houses, which were frequently able to block or delay legislation passed by the lower Houses. It was found, contrary to what had been expected, that the Councils elected on a narrow franchise (right to vote) were more conservative than the nominated ones, which could be 'swamped' with new members appointed by the Government. Queensland used this method to abolish its Legislative Council in 1922.

The remaining Legislative Councils are now elected by all people eligible to vote for the lower Houses. These reforms did not come until 1951 in Victoria, 1964 in Western Australia, 1968 in Tasmania, 1975 in

South Australia and 1978 in New South Wales. The forty-five members of the New South Wales Legislative Council are now elected for nine-year terms, fifteen members retiring in rotation every three years (or when there is an election for the lower House). Members in Victoria and South Australia are elected for six years, half the members retiring every three years. In Western Australia, since 1987, members of the Legislative Council are all elected at the same time for four-year terms. In Tasmania, the nineteen members of the Legislative Council hold their seats for six years, three retiring annually in rotation, except for the sixth year, when four retire.

The Legislative Councils of all States have used their powers to block legislation, and in Victoria and Tasmania have even caused the downfall of Governments by rejecting money Bills (Bills to authorise the spending of government funds for some purpose, such as to pay public servants). Some of the Councils are, in fact, more powerful than the House of Lords is in England, as the Lords can no longer hold up legislation indefinitely or reject money Bills. Although the Councils are now popularly elected, some have remained conservative, mainly because of the arrangement of electoral boundaries and the staggering of elections.

There are two important limitations to the power of the New South Wales Legislative Council. First, it cannot reject the annual appropriation Bills arising from the Budget, and so force a Government to a premature election. Second, the Government can put any Bill to a referendum if the Council rejects it. If it is passed in referendum it automatically becomes law.

Many people believe that an upper House should not have the power to frustrate the will of the people's representatives in the lower House—or that there is no need for an upper House at all. However, it can be reasonably argued that it is worth having an upper House as 'house of review'—to have another look at legislation before it becomes law. Members of a second chamber, being fewer in number, have more time to examine a Bill more carefully and perhaps more calmly. It is possible to improve legislation without obstructing it. Often the Government itself finds it desirable to make changes after a Bill has been passed in the lower House, and can introduce the alterations in the upper House. Most of the democratic countries of the world still have two houses of Parliament.

Labor Party policy has been to abolish the Legislative Councils, but only in Queensland was a Labor Government able to do so, in 1922. The New South Wales Legislative Council cannot be abolished unless a majority of voters agree to a referendum; one in 1961 was defeated. (In Queensland, a Legislative Council could not be restored without a referendum.) In other States, the Councils would have to agree to their own abolition; there is little chance of that so long as the Labor Party cannot win a majority there. Even then, the Labor Party is likely to be content with electoral reform.

FEDERAL PARLIAMENT

Both Houses of Federal Parliament are elected by all Australian citizens, men and women, who have reached the minimum voting age, which was reduced from twenty-one to eighteen in 1973. (There are some minor qualifications, which are explained in Chapter 6.) Anyone entitled to vote is also entitled to stand for election to either House.

A view of the new Parliament House, Canberra.

THE HOUSE OF REPRESENTATIVES

Australia is at present divided into 147 electorates, each with more or less an equal number of voters. A representative is elected from each electorate. The number of representatives from each State, therefore, depends on its population and may vary from time to time, except that no State is to have fewer than five representatives. The Australian Capital Territory elects two members and the Northern Territory one. Until 1966 and 1968 respectively, these members could vote only on certain matters affecting their territory. Elections for the House of Representatives must be held every three years, but may be held sooner.

The Constitution provides that there should be about twice as many members of the House of Representatives as there are members of the Senate. In a referendum in May 1967, electors in all States rejected a proposal to drop this requirement, and thus blocked a plan to increase the membership of the House of Representatives without enlarging the Senate. The first Federal Parliament had seventy-five members of the House of Representatives and thirty-six Senators.

In 1984, the number of Senators was increased to seventy-six, including four from the Territories. This enabled the House of Representatives to be expanded from 125 to 148. After a redistribution in 1991, the number was reduced to 147.

STATE OF THE PARTIES IN COMMONWEALTH AND STATE PARLIAMENTS, 1 JULY 1993

Commonwealth (ALP Government)

House of Representatives		Senate	
Australian Labor Party	80	Australian Labor Party	30
Liberal Party	49	Liberal Party	31
National Party	16	National Party	4
Independents	2	Country–Liberal Party (NT)	1
		Australian Democrats	7
		Greens (WA)	2
		Independent (Tas)	1

New South Wales (Liberal–National Party Government)

Legislative Assembly		Legislative Council	
Liberal Party	31	Liberal Party	13
National Party	17	National Party	7
Australian Labor Party	47	Australian Labor Party	18
Independents	4	Australian Democrats	2
		Call to Australia Party	2

Victoria (Liberal–National Party Government)

Legislative Assembly		Legislative Council	
Liberal Party	52	Liberal Party	24
National Party	9	National Party	6
Australian Labor Party	27	Australian Labor Party	14

Queensland (ALP Government)

Legislative Assembly	
Australian Labor Party	54
National Party	26
Liberal Party	9

South Australia (Liberal Government)

House of Assembly		Legislative Council	
Liberal Party	22	Liberal Party	10
Australian Labor Party	21	Australian Labor Party	10
National Party	1	Australian Democrats	2
Independents	3		

Western Australia (Liberal–National Party Government)

Legislative Assembly		Legislative Council	
Liberal Party	26	Liberal Party	13
National Party	6	National Party	3
Australian Labor Party	24	Australian Labor Party	16
Independent	1	Independent	1

Tasmania (Liberal Government)

House of Assembly		Legislative Council	
Liberal Party	19	Liberal Party	1
Australian Labor Party	11	Australian Labor Party	1
Independents (Greens)	3	Independents	17

Northern Territory (Country–Liberal Party Government)

Legislative Assembly	
Country–Liberal Party	14
Australian Labor Party	9
Independents	2

Australian Capital Territory (ALP Ministry)

Legislative Assembly	
Australian Labor Party	8
Liberal Party	6
Independents	3

THE SENATE

The founders of Federation had two purposes in mind in establishing the Senate. First, like other upper Houses, the Senate was to be a chamber of review. Second, like the Senate of the United States, it was to represent the interests of the States as equal partners in Federation. Each State, regardless of its population, was given an equal number of Senators. Originally there were six from each State; in 1948 the number was increased to ten and in 1984 to twelve. Since 1975, there have also been two Senators each from the Australian Capital Territory and Northern Territory, elected for three-year terms. To give the Senate an element of continuity as in most of the State upper Houses, Senators from the States are elected for a term of six years, but half the number from each State retire every three years.

The Senate has not, however, fulfilled the founders' expectations that it would be a *States' House*. Senators are nearly always elected as members of political parties, and usually vote according to party policy. However, the interests of the smaller States may be strongly upheld by their Senators at policy-making meetings of the parliamentary parties.

Three developments have increased the importance, independence and power of the Senate in recent years. First, from 1967 to 1975, and since 1981, no Government had a majority in the Senate. The balance was held by Democratic Labor Party and/or Independent Senators. These Senators occasionally voted with the Opposition to block Government measures. Even before 1967, some Government Senators occasionally opposed or helped to defeat Government legislation. Since July 1993 the balance of power in the Senate has been held by seven Australian Democrats, two Western Australian Greens and one Tasmanian Independent.

A second significant change has been the introduction of a system of Senate standing and select committees. Seven standing committees have been appointed to examine proposed legislation and other matters referred to them by the Senate. Each specialises in a particular area of government:

- community affairs;
- employment, education and training;
- environment, recreation and the arts;
- finance and public administration;
- foreign affairs, defence and trade;
- industry, science and technology;
- legal and constitutional affairs;
- rural and regional affairs;
- transport, communications and infrastructure.

Then there are two legislative scrutiny committees. The first examines all regulations and ordinances made by the Government under Acts of Parliament. On its recommendations, the Senate has disallowed a number of regulations and forced departments to revise others. The other, newer committee examines all Bills to ensure that they do not trespass unduly on personal rights and liberties. There are also six estimates committees, which enable Senators to keep a check on Government spending and question senior officials responsible for administering policy. Select committees are appointed from time to time (also by the House of Representatives or jointly) to look into national problems, such as water and air pollution, drug abuse, medical and hospital costs, control of stock exchanges, civil rights of immigrants, print media ownership, and super-annuation. They have power to hold public hearings and compel witnesses to attend if necessary.

The third major development arose from the political crisis of late 1975. The Senate showed that not only could it review and reject legislation but it could bring about the downfall of a Government by blocking Supply (refusing to pass appropriation Bills to authorise Government spending). As the Senate has always had the power to reject any Bill passed by the House of Representatives, deadlocks have some-times arisen between the two Houses. The Constitution provides a means of overcoming such a situation. If the Senate refuses to pass a disputed Bill a second time after an interval of three months, the Government may ask the Governor-General to dissolve both Houses. This means an immediate election must be held for each House. If, after the election the Senate again rejects the Bill, a joint sitting of the two Houses may be held, and the Bill will be passed if it is supported by an absolute majority of members of both Houses voting together.

There have been six double dissolutions since Federation. In 1914 and 1951, the new Government won a majority in both Houses, so that no joint sitting was necessary. But in 1974, the Labor Government did not gain a majority in the Senate, and an historic joint sitting was held to pass six Bills previously rejected by the Senate. The double dissolution in 1975 was different—and ominous. This time the Senate not only rejected several ordinary Bills but also refused to pass Supply with the aim of forcing the Labor Government to resign and face an election which the Opposition believed it would lose. Previously the Senate had always respected the convention that Governments are made or unmade in the lower House and that the upper House should not block Supply. In the ensuing crisis, in which the Government refused to resign and the Opposition in the Senate continued to defer consideration of the Supply Bills, the Governor-General intervened. He dismissed the Government, appointed the Opposition Leader as head of a caretaker administration and dissolved both Houses of Parliament.

AUSTRALIAN UPPER HOUSES OF PARLIAMENT, JULY 1993

	No of. members	Length of terms	Elections	Electorates	System of voting
Federal (Senate)	76	(a) Six years (b) Three years	(a) Five Senators from each State retire every three years (b) Four Senators from the Territories retire every three years	(a) Each State is one electorate returning ten Senators (b) The ACT and NT each return two Senators	Optional PR
NSW (Legislative Council)	45	Three terms of Legislative Assembly	Fifteen retire every election	Whole State as single electorate	Optional PR
Victoria (Legislative Council)	44	Two terms of Legislative Assembly	Half retire every election	Twenty-two two-member provinces	Pref.
South Australia (Legislative Council)	22	Two terms of Legislative Assembly	Half retire every election	Whole State as single electorate	Optional PR (voluntary enrolment)
Western Australia (Legislative Council)	34	Four years	All retire every four years	Two seven-member and four five-member regions	Pref.
Tasmania (Legislative Council)	19	Six years	Three retire every year (four every sixth year)	Nineteen single-member districts	Pref.

This crisis has set a precedent. In future, any Government without a majority in the Senate is at risk of being forced to an election it does not want through a refusal to pass, or threat to refuse, Supply in the Senate. The Senate is thus potentially more powerful than the House of Representatives. The Senate can force the House of Representatives to an election, but the House of Representatives cannot force an obstructive Senate to an election, except through the deadlock provisions for a double

The House of Representatives in session in the new Parliament.

dissolution. When the Senate blocks Supply, use of the deadlock provisions would take too long to resolve the crisis.

The Life of a Parliament

On 13 March 1993 the people of Australia elected their thirty-seventh Federal Parliament. The life of a Parliament in this sense means the duration of the House of Representatives from the time it is summoned by the Governor-General after a general election until it is dissolved before the next election. Under the Constitution, the maximum life of a Parliament is fixed at three years, but the House of Representatives may be dissolved sooner. This means an election must be held every three years, if it is not held earlier. The Constitution also insists that Parliament must meet at least every year.

The life of each Parliament may be divided into a number of sessions. Sometimes a session lasts the life of a Parliament, but there may be two, three, or more sessions. To end a session without dissolving Parliament, the Governor-General may prorogue Parliament. This suspends the sittings, and all unfinished business is cancelled. Any Bill still to be dealt with when Parliament is prorogued (or dissolved) has to be introduced again at a later session, or else it lapses. Usually the date of the opening of the next session is proclaimed at the time of prorogation.

Either House of Parliament may adjourn for varying periods—from one day to the next, or for a week, or for a longer time, such as for a summer or winter recess. Any business before the House can be continued when the House meets again.

To sum up: *dissolution* ends the life of a Parliament (that is, the lower House) before an election; *prorogation* ends a session without dissolution; and *adjournment* suspends a sitting of either House without 'wiping off' unfinished business.

The Crown, represented by the Governor-General, normally on the advice of the Government, summons, dissolves or prorogues Parliament; the Speaker of the House of Representatives and the President of the Senate, usually at the request of the Government or on the resolution of the House, adjourn and recall their respective Houses.

The procedure is similar in the State Parliaments. The maximum life of the State Parliaments (the Lower Houses) is now four years in all States except Queensland, where it is three years.

PARLIAMENTARY SOVEREIGNTY

In Britain, Parliament has absolute sovereignty. Its powers are supreme and unlimited: it can make or unmake any law. If it wished, it could abolish the monarchy, or set up a dictatorship, or take away all civil liberties. There is no written Constitution or law to prevent these things. But Parliament does not use its powers in this way. The women and men elected to it legislate in accordance with established practice and tradition, respecting the rule of law and remembering their responsibility to the people whom they represent.

The Australian Parliaments are not sovereign in the British sense. The Federal Parliament is limited by the Constitution. Parliament may legislate only within the limits of the powers given to it by the Constitution; if it exceeds those powers, its action can be challenged in the High Court, which can declare a law so made to be invalid. The State Parliaments are also restricted. They may make laws only on those subjects which are not expressly reserved for the Federal Parliament.

For further thought

- There is an old saying: 'If an upper House agrees with the lower House, it is superfluous; it if disagrees, it is obnoxious.' What do you think?
- Should the Legislative Councils stay as they are, be reformed, or be abolished? If you think they should be reformed, what changes do you suggest? (See also Chapter 6 on elections.)
- Does the Senate serve a useful function as a House representing the interests of the States?
- Should the Senate have the power to force a Government to face an election by refusing to grant Supply?
- Would it be desirable and practicable to have an upper House which represents various vocational or economic interest groups in the community? How could or should such a House be chosen? Should it be able to veto legislation or merely act as an advisory body?

CHAPTER

4

CABINET GOVERNMENT

For many centuries the Kings and Queens of England have not been able to change the law without the 'advice and consent' of Parliament. As time passed, laws came to be made in Parliament without the presence of the Sovereign who gave assent as a matter of course. Just as the role of the Sovereign as head of the legislature has become purely formal, so has the position as head of the executive. Today the Queen reigns; she does not rule. Nor does a Governor-General rule. Government is in the hands of a group of Ministers known as the Cabinet, whose leader is the Prime Minister.

Minister is Latin for servant, and Ministers were originally royal servants who advised the King on important affairs of state and made sure that the laws were carried out. In the early seventeenth century, the King usually summoned his council of close advisers privately in his cabinet, or royal apartment. This council became known as the *Cabinet Council*, or simply as the Cabinet.

From 1714, when the Georges of Hanover occupied the British throne, the Cabinet became more important. King George I did not speak English, and was more concerned with the affairs of Hanover than with those of his new kingdom. So he left his Cabinet to meet alone. But as he could not raise money for government without Parliament, he had to rely on Ministers who gained the support of Parliament. So important was the 'power of the purse' that the Treasurer became the principal adviser, or Prime Minister, to the King. Sir Robert Walpole, who controlled the Treasury from 1721 to 1742, was in effect Britain's first Prime Minister (although he did not like the term).

During the eighteenth century, the Cabinet grew in power. The King chose a Prime Minister who could fill Cabinet from his supporters in

Parliament. Each Minister was given charge of one or more of the departments of government. To strengthen their position, Ministers agreed to 'stick together' and take joint responsibility for their decisions and actions. By the time Queen Victoria came to the throne, the Prime Minister and his Cabinet had come to depend more on the support of the majority of members of Parliament than on the support of the Sovereign.

Australia adopted the Cabinet system as part of the British heritage of parliamentary government, a system that developed over some 300 years. Its essential feature is that the Government—the Cabinet or Ministry—is chosen from the party or combination of parties having a majority of members in the lower House of Parliament. The Government stays in office so long as it keeps that majority.

The Cabinet system has been followed by many other democratic countries. The other major system of executive government is the presidential, of which the best known is that of the United States. There, the people indirectly elect a chief executive as President, who can choose as heads of the Administration anyone who is not a member of Congress (Parliament). Whereas in the British system members of the Government *must* be members of Parliament, in the American system they *must not* be. It sometimes happens in America that a President and the majority of members of Congress belong to opposing political parties.

FEDERAL CABINET IN AUSTRALIA

This is how the Cabinet system works in Australia: Let us suppose a general election has just been held for Federal Parliament, and that one party has won a majority (more than half the seats) in the House of Representatives. As we shall see in the next two chapters, most if not all members of Parliament are members of political parties. The Governor-General, as the Queen's representative, sends for the leader of the successful party (or combination of parties), and asks the leader to form a Ministry to govern the country. The leader submits a list of supporters in Parliament to act as the Cabinet or Ministry with the leader as Prime Minister. The Governor-General then formally appoints them as 'Her Majesty's Ministers of State for Australia'.

Most Ministers take charge of one or more departments, or are responsible for sections of a department. The number of Ministers and departments has grown over the years, and their titles have changed with widening scope and shifting emphasis of government activity. In the first ten years of Federal Government there were only eight to ten Ministers and seven departments. In recent years, there has been a tendency to amalgamate departments into bigger units and have more than one Minister sharing responsibility for them.

In July 1993, the Labor Government led by Paul Keating had thirty Ministers, the first nineteen forming the Cabinet and the others the 'outer Ministry'. Together they were in charge of eighteen departments. Some senior Ministers were also assisted by parliamentary secretaries, who are members of Parliament without ministerial rank. The Keating Cabinet consisted of the Prime Minister; Deputy Prime Minister (also Minister for Housing, Local Government and Community Services); Government Leader in the Senate (also Foreign Affairs); Deputy Leader in the Senate (also Defence); Treasurer; Attorney-General; and Ministers for Finance; Trade; Employment, Education and Training; Environment, Sport and Territories; Transport and Communications; Immigration and Ethnic Affairs; Primary Industry and Energy; Industry, Technology and Regional Development; Industrial Relations (also Arts and Administrative Services); Tourism (also Resources); Health; and Social Security.

The 'outer Ministry' consisted of the Assistant Treasurer; Special Minister of State; and Ministers for Schools, Vocational Education and Training; Communications; Justice; Aboriginal and Torres Strait Islanders' Affairs; Development Cooperation and Pacific Island Affairs; Family Services; Veterans' Affairs (also Defence Science and Personnel); and Science and Small Business. Ministers are ranked in order of precedence according to their seniority or status in the party, not according to the importance of their portfolio. Some Ministers had the additional responsibility of assisting the Prime Minister or other senior Ministers, or representing them in the other chamber.

Each Minister is *individually* responsible to Parliament for the policy and actions of his or her department, and all the Ministers are *collectively* responsible for the policy of the Government as a whole. The Ministers meet privately in Cabinet, usually once a week when Parliament is sitting, to discuss matters of policy and ways of putting them into effect. Each Minister may speak freely at these secret meetings, but once a decision is taken, each Minister is bound by it and equally responsible for it. However, the convention that a Minister who cannot agree with an important Cabinet decision should resign is not always followed.

Most Governments make a distinction between the Ministry and the Cabinet. When the number of Ministers is considered too big for them all to function efficiently as a committee, only the most important and senior Ministers are admitted to the Cabinet, the others being called in only when their departments are concerned.

In Labor Governments, the Cabinet is elected by ballot in a caucus (party meeting) of all the Labor members of Parliament, but the Prime Minister (or State Premier) allots the Ministerial portfolios. The Federal

Liberal Party has followed the British tradition of leaving it to the Prime Minister to pick his Cabinet, although in a coalition the National Party nominates its Ministers. After the March 1993 election, Mr Keating was given unprecedented authority for a Labor Prime Minister to choose the team that he wanted rather than have the Ministry imposed on him by caucus and its factions.

Whether selected by the party leader or caucus, Ministers are supposedly chosen from among the most senior, experienced or able members in the governing party or coalition. Normally other influences also come into play. The composition of Labor Party Ministries often depends on the balance of power among party factions, while the leader's personal preferences may play an important role in the formation of a Liberal or Liberal–National Party coalition Government. Care is also taken to ensure that all States are fairly represented in Federal Cabinet, that there is a reasonable balance between city and country members, and that some women are chosen as Ministers.

Although the Government is formed from the majority in the lower House, some Ministers are normally chosen from the upper House. The Federal Ministry in 1993 included eight Senators. The Prime Minister, by custom, always sits in the House of Representatives. If a majority party chooses a leader from the Senate, as the Liberal Party did in electing Mr John Gorton in 1968, then he has to win a seat in the House of Representatives as soon as he can.

STATE CABINETS

The leader of each of the State Cabinets is the Premier. The leaders of the Northern Territory and Australian Capital Territory are called Chief Minister. State Cabinets range in membership from ten in Tasmania to twenty in New South Wales and twenty-two in Victoria. Ministers may have more than one portfolio, and titles vary from State to State. In Victoria, the Government led by Jeff Kennett in July 1993 had a record number of twenty-two Ministers in charge of only thirteen 'super' departments, with up to four Ministers sharing responsibility for each department. The Victorian Cabinet consisted of the Premier (also Minister for Ethnic Affairs), Deputy Premier (also Police and Emergency Services, Tourism, and Corrections), Government Leader in the Legislative Council (also Conservation and Environment, and Major Projects), Deputy Leader in the Council (also Arts, Tertiary Education and Training, and Gaming), Treasurer, Attorney-General (also Fair Trading and Women's Affairs) and Ministers for Agriculture, Roads and Ports, Regional Development and Local Government (also WorkCover),

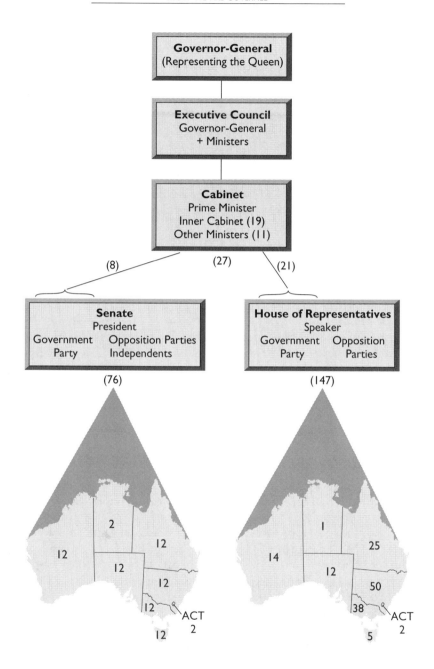

Federal Parliament and Government

Industry and Employment, Natural Resources, Education, Planning, Health Services, Energy and Minerals, Housing and Aged Care, Industry Services, Sport, Recreation and Racing, Public Transport, Small Business (also Youth Affairs), Community Services (also Aboriginal Affairs), and Finance.

THE EXECUTIVE COUNCIL

In Britain the rules that the Queen should act on the advice of her Ministers, that Ministers must be Members of Parliament having the support of the majority party in the lower House, and that Ministers are individually and collectively responsible to Parliament, are not laid down by law. These unwritten rules of practice, known as *conventions*, are however, observed as strictly as any Act of Parliament. Australian Cabinets, too, work largely by convention—there is no mention of Cabinet in the Federal or State Constitutions—but the appointment and payment of Ministers is governed by law.

MINISTERS IN AUSTRALIAN PARLIAMENTS, JULY 1993									
	Federal	*NSW*	*Vic*	*Qld*	*SA*	*WA*	*Tas*	*NT*	*ACT*	*Total*
Upper House	8	3	5	-	3	5	-	-	-	24
Lower House	22	17	17	18	10	12	10	9	4	119
Total	30	20	22	18	13	17	10	9	4	143

The supreme executive authority of government, as we have seen, is vested in the Queen, who is represented in Australia by a Governor-General and six State Governors, each of whom has an Executive Council to advise him or her. (In Britain the Queen's advisers are members of the Privy Council.) The Executive Council consists of the Governor-General or Governor and the Cabinet Ministers of the day. Cabinet meetings, where government policy and action are discussed and decided, are private and secret. Meetings of the Executive Council are formal and official, and give legal form, where necessary, to decisions of Cabinet. The Governor-General or Governor (or the deputy) presides, and only two Ministers need be present as well. At these meetings proclamations are issued, appointments to public office are made, and regulations authorised by Acts of Parliament are approved. These are legally said to be made by the Governor-General-in-Council or Governor-in-Council.

COALITIONS

The Cabinet system seems to work best where there are only two major political parties in Parliament. Since the rise of a third important party in Australia—the National (formerly Country) Party—it often happens after an election that no single party has a majority to enable it to form a Government alone. This problem has been resolved in either of two ways. Either one party governs as a minority Government with the support of another party or Independent member, or else two parties form a coalition with Ministers from each party.

Coalitions have long been a feature of non-Labor Federal Governments. From 1949 to 1972 and from 1975 to 1983, the Liberal and National (Country) Parties formed joint Cabinets, although the Ministers to some extent remained responsible to their own parties and each party continued to operate more or less independently inside and outside Parliament. The two parties now also work together as a coalition in Opposition.

The present NSW Government is a coalition of the Liberal and National parties, and has to rely on Independents for a majority in the Legislative Assembly. The Victorian Government elected in October 1992 is also a coalition, formed while in Opposition, although the Liberal Party won sufficient seats to govern alone. In the past ten years, former Labor Governments in South Australia, Western Australia and Tasmania have had to rely on Independents—either elected as such or parliamentary members who resigned from the governing party over some disagreement—to be able to govern. Such Governments tend to be unstable.

From the 1920s to 1950s, the Country Party at times governed Victoria with the support of either Labor or the major non-Labor party, even if it was itself the smallest party in Parliament. Such arrangements tended to be short-lived. Victoria had fifty-nine Governments and thirty-nine Premiers in a century, its shortest Government (in 1943) having lasted only five days. New South Wales in 1921 had the shortest Government on record—a Ministry which lasted only seven hours.

THE OPPOSITION

The majority party or combination of parties in the lower House of Parliament forms the Government; the remaining party, or biggest of the remaining parties or coalition of parties becomes the Opposition. The Opposition is an essential part of our parliamentary democracy. In a dictatorship no opposition is tolerated, and in some countries its freedom to speak or act is severely restricted. In Australia, the Opposition is not only free but is indeed expected to criticise Government-sponsored legislation, to ask questions about the Government's administration, and to point out failures and omissions.

The Opposition is, in short, the alternative Government. If a Government becomes unpopular, the people at the next elections may give the Opposition party enough votes for a majority and so enable it to replace the Government. Today's Leader of the Opposition thus becomes tomorrow's Prime Minister. The Opposition usually has a *shadow Cabinet*, a group of senior members who can serve as Ministers should their party or coalition be elected to power.

CABINET AND PARLIAMENT

So far, we have been making a distinction between the legislative and executive functions of government—between making the laws and putting them into effect. We have looked at Parliament as the legislature and Cabinet as the executive. In the United States, the two functions are strictly separated, but not in the British and Australian systems.

Cabinet has become, in the words of the great political writer of the nineteenth century, Walter Bagehot, 'a hyphen which joins, a buckle which fastens' the legislative part of government to the executive part. Nearly all Bills these days are introduced in Parliament by the Government. Cabinet decides what the laws shall be and when they are to be introduced.

All Bills to authorise the spending of government money must be introduced in the form of a recommendation from the Governor-General or Governor—in effect, they must come from Cabinet. Parliament may debate, find fault and suggest amendments, but a determined Government, able to control the timetable of the House and to rely on the party loyalty of its supporters, is bound to get its way. In theory, laws are made by the Queen in Parliament; in fact, laws are made by Cabinet in Parliament.

Is, then, the role of Parliament merely that of a 'rubber stamp' to approve decisions of the Government? No, not necessarily so. Parliament from its ranks provides a Government, but it also provides an Opposition. The Government governs; the Opposition criticises, queries and expounds opposite points of view. Parliament is, or should be, a forum where all manner of public affairs may be freely discussed and brought to the people's attention, where the Government collectively and Ministers individually are held openly accountable for their policies and administration, where injustices and grievances may be exposed to public notice.

Despite the Government's control over parliamentary proceedings, there are still plenty of opportunities for Parliament to fulfil these functions. At *question time* the Ministers may be called on to justify their actions or those of their departments. Members may move *motions to discuss a matter of urgent importance*; the Opposition may bring down *censure motions* to attack the Government; and on a Minister's *motion to adjourn* the day's sitting, members may speak on any matter they choose. On *special occasions*, such as the 'address-in-reply' debate which follows the Governor-General's or Governor's opening speech, and on budget debates, members may criticise any aspect of the Government's policy and administration.

Parliamentary committees—formed in either House or jointly—can do valuable work in scrutinising Government accounts and proposals for public works to prevent waste and extravagant spending, and they can safeguard the citizen against unnecessary official interference by reviewing legislation and regulations. Some standing committees specialise in particular subjects over which they keep a regular watch, and select committees are appointed from time to time to inquire into matters of public concern. Such committees can be given powers to call witnesses, demand documents and punish people who refuse to cooperate.

General debates on legislation, even when it is known beforehand how each member will vote, have their worth. For in this way the people may be made aware of what the Government is doing or not doing, and what the Opposition proposes to do if it gains power. The people are thus better able to record their approval or disapproval of the Government at election time.

For further thought

- What are the advantages and disadvantages of the Cabinet system as compared with the American presidential system?
- 'The duty of the Opposition is to oppose.' Why is that an inadequate definition of the functions of the Opposition?
- Has the executive become too powerful at the expense of the legislature? If so, how can the balance be restored?

POLITICAL PARTIES

Parliamentary government as we know it could not work without political parties. Parliament needs at least two parties, the one holding a majority to form a Government and the minority one to be the Opposition. There can be more than two parties, but preferably not many more. Even three or four parties in Parliament, when none has a clear majority, may mean frequent changes of Ministries. This tends to make for unstable and irresponsible government.

The party system and the cabinet system developed side by side in England, and have come to depend on one another. Parties were originally groups of men of similar views who acted together in Parliament for common purposes. After 1680, the English Parliament was divided into two parties, the Whigs and the Tories. The Whigs wanted to limit the authority of the King and give more power to Parliament; the Tories, many of them supporters of the ill-fated Stuart Kings, believed that royal authority should be upheld. Whig and Tory were at first terms of abuse. The Whigs were named for a set of Scottish rebels and the Tories for gangs of Irish robbers. But the names stuck for 150 years, when the parties, by then rather different in character, adopted the names of Liberal and Conservative.

It was about this time that the parties developed their modern form. In the eighteenth century, they were still loosely linked groups of parliamentarians centring on a few leading personalities or powerful families. But during the nineteenth century, as more and more people were given the right to vote, the parties became organised, not only within Parliament, but also among the electors, whose support they endeavoured to win.

A modern political party in Australia is not merely a group of likeminded Members of Parliament. It is an organisation of people of broadly similar ideas or interests, whose aim is to gain political power. A party tries to win power by having as many of its members as possible elected to Parliament. If it can get enough members elected for a majority in the lower House, it will be able to form a Government. Members of a party are more or less agreed on what the tasks of government should be and how they should be carried out. They want to govern so that they can achieve their objectives. At the same time, they may wish to prevent their opponents, whose ideas they believe to be wrong or whose interests are contrary to their own, from gaining or maintaining power.

Even if a party cannot get enough members elected to be able to govern, it may be able to influence the Government by gaining the balance of power. For example, when there are three parties in Parliament and none can govern by itself, the third party has the balance of power and can decide which of the other two it will enable to form a Government, and what concessions it will ask for as the price of its support.

A person need not be a member of a political party to stand for Parliament, but Independents—candidates not 'endorsed' by a party—are seldom elected. By an exceptional tradition, most members of the Tasmanian Legislative Council are Independents, because the Liberal Party normally does not endorse candidates for Council elections. Only a party can govern, and most people want to vote for or against a Government. An elector may vote for a particular candidate, because he or she believes that candidate to be a better or abler person. However, the elector is more likely to ask, not 'which person would I rather see in Parliament?' but 'which party would I rather see in power?', although the choice may be influenced as much by the personality or ability of the leader of the party as by the party's policy.

Political parties perform two important functions in a parliamentary democracy such as ours. First, they select candidates to stand for Parliament. Second, they put forward alternative policies. The voter simply has to choose. The parties, of course, do more than offer a choice—they try to influence that choice. Not content with naming candidates, they campaign vigorously to get them elected. Not merely do they formulate policies reflecting the needs and demands of their followers but they select, stir up and organise issues to win them a wider support.

Each party likes to give the impression that its members are united in their aims, but anyone who follows the news realises that this is not usually so. The parties, as well as competing with one another for public support, are themselves in continual ferment. There are formal factions or informal groupings of various interests and viewpoints struggling to influence their party's course, and of ambitious individuals jockeying for position or power within the party structure. These internal conflicts are normal, but they can be damaging if they become too extreme or bitter, leading to loss of public confidence or party splits.

Australia has three major political parties with experience in governing: the Australian Labor Party (ALP), the Liberal Party, and the National Party (NP). The names of the two non-Labor parties have varied from time to time and State to State, although in recent years divisions have become more blurred.

The Australian parties have been traditionally based on economic or class interests in the community. The Australian Labor Party gets most of its members and votes from among trade unionists and other workers, who look to governments to help them gain higher wages, better working conditions, more social services and cheaper housing. The Liberal Party gains its strongest support from business people, property owners, professionals and many 'white-collar' workers—'middle-class' people of whom many desire lower taxation, less government spending and encouragement to private enterprise. The National Party is supported mainly by farmers and graziers and people living in country towns, who want better amenities for the country and organised marketing of farm products to maintain good prices. But none of the parties can rely entirely on the support of any particular interest or group of people. Many wage-earners vote Liberal or National Party rather than Labor, many business people vote Labor instead of Liberal, and many farmers do not support the National Party. Then there are the 'swinging' or 'floating' voters, who change their minds between elections, and those who vote for other minority parties.

Each party must therefore appeal to many different sorts of people for its support. The parties present themselves as national rather than sectional in outlook and programme, and claim to promote policies that will benefit the State or nation as a whole.

Anyone can become a member of a political party by joining the local branch of the party of his or her choice and paying a membership fee. Members are expected to attend branch meetings and at election time to do all they can to ensure that the party's candidate is elected to Parliament. The major parties also have separate organisations for women and for young people, providing a social as well as a political fellowship.

The branches send delegates to State conferences, which meet at regular intervals, perhaps once or twice a year, to discuss matters of policy. Decisions requiring legislative or Government action are referred to the party's parliamentary members. Between conference meetings, each party organisation is controlled by a State executive or council, which usually has permanent city offices and paid officials. The parties may also

An election campaign meeting, country-style.

have electoral councils in each electorate to help select candidates for Parliament and to help organise their campaigns.

The parties are organised separately in each State, and not only their names but also their policies may vary slightly from State to State. Each State organisation sends delegates to a Federal council or conference and to small Federal executives. The Liberal Party, ALP and NP have Federal offices in Canberra. The party organisations have considerable influence on their parliamentary representatives, particularly in the case of the ALP. On the other hand, a strong parliamentary leader may be a powerful figure in the 'outside' party organisation.

Each of the parties exerts a certain amount of discipline on its parliamentary members. The ALP requires every parliamentary candidate to uphold the party's principles and to vote in Parliament as the majority of the parliamentary party decides in a caucus meeting. A Labor member can try to influence the party's policy in caucus, but once a majority decision is taken, the member must abide by it. The Liberal and National Parties generally do not ask for such a pledge, but any member who consistently disagrees with the party and votes against it will lose its support at elections.

Each party has a constitution, setting out its structure, body of rules and basic beliefs and principles, and a 'platform', setting out its objectives and policies.

The main political parties in Australia do not differ as much in their policies as one would suppose from their election speeches or statements in Parliament. One reason is that neither side can afford to stray too far from what most people would regard as fair and tolerable. Another is that at times of economic difficulty neither Governments nor Oppositions can ignore the importance of good economic management, or afford to make or fulfil lavish promises. Often the parties differ only in their emphasis, priorities or methods.

The five planks of the Labor Party's first Federal platform—adult suffrage, restricted immigration, age pensions, arbitration for industrial disputes, and national defence—became generally adopted and accepted by all parties as basic to Australian society. But in the past twenty years or so, three of these objectives have been revised on both sides of politics. Restricted immigration no longer means racial discrimination as it originally did, when Australia openly and offensively followed a 'White Australia' policy.

The main parties still believe in social security for those in need, but now there is an increasing emphasis on superannuation based on employer (and perhaps employee) contributions to provide for those who retire from work. Support for centralised arbitration and wage-fixing has been eroded by moves towards enterprise bargaining. However, the

Labor and non-Labor parties differ on such questions as the size and nature of the immigration intake; whether superannuation should be compulsory or voluntary; and how enterprise bargaining should work. Both sides have also moved away from their former policies of protecting the manufacturing industry against imports with high tariffs and restrictions.

In the 1970s, all parties showed a greater concern for 'quality of life' issues: the problems of urban and suburban living; the protection of the environment against pollution and 'development'; and the protection of consumers against dishonest business practices. Towards the end of the decade and through the 1980s, economic circumstances forced Governments and Oppositions to give priority to problems of inflation and unemployment, financial deregulation, industrial relations and welfare policies, and the development of Australian mineral resources. In the early 1990s, as a result of a severe economic recession and unfavourable trade conditions, the emphasis turned towards encouraging industry to become more competitive, productive and export-minded; making the public service and government enterprises more efficient and cost-effective; reducing debt; and creating jobs.

There has also been political controversy at times about 'social conscience' questions, such as censorship and abortion. On these questions, there is often wider disagreement within a party than between parties. Sometimes such conflict is resolved by a parliamentary party allowing its members to vote according to their conscience rather than on party lines.

THE AUSTRALIAN LABOR PARTY

In Britain the Labour Party is the youngest of the big national parties, but in Australia it is the oldest party with a continuous history. It grew out of the rapidly expanding trade union movement in the late nineteenth century. Particularly after the failure of the great maritime and shearers' strikes in 1890 and 1891, trade union leaders turned from industrial action to politics as a means of improving the conditions of working people. They were influenced by a small group of Socialists, who wanted to change society by bringing about a fairer distribution of the nation's wealth.

In 1891, thirty-five Labor men were elected to the New South Wales Legislative Assembly and similar successes soon followed in the other mainland colonies. In the first Federal Parliament, sixteen Labor members were elected to the House of Representatives and eight to the Senate.

Finding itself holding the balance of power, Labor used party discipline to forge a strong team in Parliament, able to bargain for what it wanted by giving or withholding its support to or from the governing party. In April 1904 Australia had its first Labor Prime Minister, J C Watson, although he was able to govern for only a few months. Labor won its first outright majority in the House of Representatives in 1910 and governed for three years with Andrew Fisher as Prime Minister. In 1918, the party adopted its present name of Australian Labor Party (ALP).

The ALP is still sometimes described as a socialist party, and some of its members regard themselves as socialists. In 1921, the party adopted as its objective the 'socialisation of industry, production, distribution and exchange'. This meant that the party believed that factories, mines, big business organisations and public transport should be owned or controlled by the government, representing the people, rather than by powerful companies conducting them for profit. This radical objective was soon qualified by a statement, known as the 'Blackburn declaration', that the party did not intend to abolish private ownership of industries or businesses that were conducted in a 'socially useful manner and without exploitation'.

This was reworded in 1957 (substantially) and 1981 (slightly) to read: 'The Australian Labor Party is a democratic socialist party and has the objective of the democratic socialisation of industry, production, distribution and exchange, to the extent necessary to eliminate exploitation and other anti-social features in these fields.' The platform lists twenty-three points for which the party stands and declares the party's belief that 'the task of building democratic socialism is a cooperative process which requires constitutional action through the Australian and State Parliaments, municipal and other statutory authorities; union action; and ongoing action by organised community groups'. This is very different from the objective of the former communist parties, which sought to abolish private ownership by revolutionary, if necessary by violent, means.

The ALP has differed also from the European Socialist parties. The founders of the ALP were practical men, more interested in action than in ideas, more eager to reform existing society than to reconstruct it. They were inspired by strong national sentiments, regarding themselves as Australians rather than as members of an international working-class. The need for support in elections from people who do not believe in socialism, and the limits imposed by the Federal Constitution, have restrained the party from carrying out most of its socialist aims.

In 1978, the then Federal leader of the ALP, Bill Hayden, described himself as a 'social democrat' rather than a socialist. By this he meant that he believed in gradual change at a pace the community could accept and the economy could bear. He thought nationalisation was a clumsy and provocative tool that would bring more political ill-will than benefit. His successors Bob Hawke and Paul Keating would also regard themselves as social democrats.

The party has often been torn by internal struggles between its left (more radical and socialist) wing and its right (more moderate) wing, but it has survived three major splits. In 1916, during the First World War, the party was sharply divided over conscription (compulsory military training and service) which the Labor Prime Minister, W.M. Hughes, wanted to introduce. Facing a revolt by most of his followers in Parliament, Hughes and his supporters left the party and later joined the Liberals to form the National Party. The second split came in 1931 during the great depression, when another senior Labor politician, J.A. Lyons, walked out of the party and joined his former opponents, the Nationalists, to form and lead the United Australia Party. The latest and most serious split came in 1954, mainly over the party's attitude to communism, and resulted in the formation of the Democratic Labor Party, which helped to keep Labor federally out of power until 1972.

Internal divisions over party policy have led to the formation of *factions*, which operate federally and within the States, as well as inside and outside the parliamentary parties. Federally, there are broadly three factions—the Right, Left and Centre Left—although some members remain unaligned. The Right, called Centre Unity in New South Wales and Victoria, supports the pragmatic approach to government of the Prime Minister, Mr Keating. They believe that to win and hold popular support, the party has to delay or modify some of its traditional policies, and argue that sound economic management must come before Labor's historic concern for social justice and equality. The Centre Left is a little more idealistic than the hard-headed Right, leaning more towards redistributive taxation and social security policies and, in foreign policy, being more qualified in its support for the American alliance. The Centre Left's main strength is in Queensland, Western Australia and South

Australia. It is loosely allied with a small but influential group of Independents.

The Left, called the Socialist Left in Victoria, is the most tightly organised of the factions, operating almost as a party within a party The Left is also the most ideological and socialist minded of the factions, often preferring to uphold socialist and egalitarian principles over the pursuit of electoral popularity, although it too has had to become more pragmatic when Labor is in power. In Victoria, a more 'hard-line' radical Pledge group has split from the Socialist Left.

Affiliated *trade unions* in each State are the mainstay of the ALP, providing most of its members and money. In addition, there are *local branches* and *electorate councils* or assemblies. The *State conference* (convention in South Australia; congress in New South Wales) is the highest governing and policy-making body of the party in each State. The conferences are made up mainly of representatives of branches or electorate councils and delegates from affiliated unions. In New South Wales and Victoria, union representation is about sixty per cent. New South Wales and South Australia also have *State councils* responsible for branch administration and policy interpretation between conferences. Each State has an *administrative committee* or State executive to manage the affairs of the State branch and give effect to conference decisions. There are also *party committees* to formulate election policies and select parliamentary candidates. The size and representation of these bodies at all levels vary from State to State.

Above the State organisations is the *national conference*, the supreme governing authority of the party, which normally meets every second year, and the *national executive*, the chief administrative authority which rules between conferences. From 1993, the conference has had 101 delegates comprising the party leaders and deputy leaders in the House of Representatives and Senate; the party leaders of each State and the Northern Territory; a Young Labor delegate; and additional delegates from each State, the Northern Territory and Australian Capital Territory, according to a formula based on the number of seats in the House of Representatives. Before 1984, the States were represented equally. The national executive consists of the four Federal parliamentary leaders and deputies, two delegates from each State, one each from the Northern Territory and Australian Capital Territory, and twelve members elected by the national conference. Each year the national executive elects the president, and a senior and two junior vice-presidents. Day-to-day administration is in the hands of the *national secretariat* headed by the national secretary, a paid official appointed by the conference. The national president attends conference and executive meetings but may vote only if also a delegate. The national secretary and assistant secretary attend these meetings but have no voting rights. State leaders may also attend executive meetings but may not vote unless they are delegates.

Decisions of the national conference are binding on every member and all sections of the party, and decisions of the national executive are binding, subject only to appeal to the conference. However, the party's constitution now limits the type of directives that the conference or executive may give the parliamentary party, and the old jibe that the ALP

The Prime Minister, Mr Paul Keating, on the election trail.

is controlled by 'faceless men' of the party machine has lost most of its point. There is also a platform review committee to resolve any conflicts over policy between the parliamentary party (caucus) and the national bodies. When Labor governs, Cabinet and caucus are generally able to set the priorities for parliamentary action.

Since the 1970s, and more especially since the early 1980s, the ALP has departed from many of its traditional policies and beliefs. It has been forced to do so mainly by economic necessity, and at the cost of much tension and dissent within its ranks and among its traditional supporters.

The end of 1972 marked a turning point with the election of the Federal Labor Government led by Gough Whitlam. Whitlam led a party which had largely healed the bitter divisions of the 1954 split and which, with its moderate and pragmatic policies and his gifts as a public speaker, won the support of many middle-class Australians. Like his predecessors, Whitlam strongly believed in the idea of equal opportunity for all Australians, and in the use of government—especially central government—intervention to ensure better education, health, housing, welfare and urban services. His Government also pursued a more independent foreign policy and the ideals of social progress, economic justice, Aboriginal rights and racial and sexual equality.

The Whitlam Government's downfall in 1975 was due not only to the crisis in the Senate and its consequent dismissal by the Governor-General, Sir John Kerr. It had also lost public confidence through its failures of economic management and lapses of ministerial discipline, which led to high budget deficits, wage inflation and unemployment. Whitlam's successors as Labor leaders—Bill Hayden (1976–83), Bob Hawke (who led Labor back to power in 1983) and Paul Keating (who replaced Hawke in 1991)—all realised that the ALP had to convince voters that it could manage the economy better than its opponents in difficult times.

The modern Labor Party is still committed to ideals of equality and opportunity (especially for women, Aboriginal people and other disadvantaged groups), the redistribution of income, wealth and economic power through taxation and social security, universal health care, full employment and the elimination of poverty. But it has come to realise more sharply that there are limits to what can be responsibly achieved through government action, regulation, borrowing and spending. While forging stronger links with the trade union movement through a wages and prices Accord, the Hawke and Keating Governments have also sought to win the confidence of business and industry through their commitment to financial deregulation, free market forces, restraint of government spending, lower rates of taxation and efforts to make the economy more competitive through lower protection, wage restraint, investment incentives, and reform of public enterprises. Labor's embrace of 'economic rationalism' at a time of recession and high unemployment has dismayed many of its traditional supporters, whose loyalty has been maintained partly by the fear of even harsher policies put forward by the non-Labor parties.

The main difference between the Labor and coalition parties during the 1993 Federal election campaign were Labor's opposition to the introduction of a broadly based goods and services tax to reduce income tax and replace other taxes as proposed by the Opposition, the nature and pace of industrial relations reform, and Labor's support for Australia's adoption by the turn of the century of a republican Constitution. The Keating Government also believes that the Commonwealth should take the lead in setting national goals, collecting revenue and managing the economy, and attaches lesser importance to the role and responsibilities of the States.

THE LIBERAL PARTY

The Liberal Party in its present form is a comparatively young party. It was founded in 1945, but its origins can be traced to groups in the early colonial and first Federal Parliaments. Unlike the Labor Party, which was formed outside Parliament mainly by the trade union movement, the forerunners of the Liberal Party were groups formed by men in Parliament who later developed party organisations to support them.

The two groups opposed to Labor in the first Federal Parliament were the Freetraders and the Protectionists. The Freetraders, strongest in New South Wales, were backed by merchants and squatters who wanted the least possible government interference in trade, commerce and industry. The Protectionists, whose stronghold was Victoria, wanted the Government to help the growth of manufacturing industries by imposing high tariffs on cheap imported goods.

In 1909 these groups joined in a 'Fusion Party' which by 1913 came to be called the Liberal Party. Under the Prime Ministership of Alfred Deakin, the Protectionists, the Fusion Party and later the Liberals, supported by the Labor Party, laid the foundations of our present system of social services (by introducing age and invalid pensions), industrial arbitration (which made possible the first basic wage), and national defence.

After the first big split in the Labor Party, Prime Minister Hughes and his followers broke away to join the Liberals and form the National Party in 1916. After the second ALP split, the Labor breakaways combined with the Nationalists to form the United Australia Party (UAP) in 1931.

The UAP, which suffered heavy defeats in elections during the war, dissolved in 1944. Some of its leaders, notably R.G. (later Sir Robert) Menzies, decided to start afresh by forming the present Liberal Party.

The Liberal Party is a loose federation of party organisations in each State and the Australian Capital Territory. In South Australia, the Liberals merged with the Country Party in 1933 in the Liberal and Country League, but reverted to the name of Liberal Party in 1973 after a separate Country Party re-emerged. In Western Australia, the Liberal Party was also formerly called the Liberal and Country League. In Victoria, the Liberal Party called itself the Liberal and Country Party when a number of Country Party breakaways joined it in 1948, but dropped the words 'and Country' in 1965.

Each of the State and Australian Capital Territory Divisions of the party is made up of local branches, women's sections and Young Liberal branches. The policy-making body of each Division is the State council (convention in Queensland, conference in Western Australia). State executives (administrative committee in Victoria) manage the party organisation between council meetings. Victoria also has a larger policy assembly which meets every month.

The Liberal Party's *Federal council* of sixty-four delegates brings together representatives from each division, including State parliamentary leaders, the Federal parliamentary leadership, and the Federal office-bearers. The council's structure reflects the Federal nature of the party.

Each State Division has eight members and the ACT four. The Northern Territory Country–Liberal Party sends an observer. The Federal executive of eighteen comprises the officers (president, two vice-presidents and treasurer), the Federal parliamentary and Senate leaders and deputy leaders of the party. Each State Division has an equal number of delegates, while the Australian Capital Territory has half that number, and the Northern Territory Country–Liberal Party has observer status. The *Federal executive* of eighteen comprises the officers (president, two vice-presidents and treasurer), the Federal parliamentary leader, deputy and Senate leader, one delegate (usually the president) from each Division, the president of the Federal women's committee, two Young Liberals, and the immediate past president. The party has a *Federal secretariat*, headed by a director in Canberra and a staff of research and public relations experts.

In contrast to the ALP, the Liberal Party's Federal organisation has no control over the State Divisions, and decisions of neither the Federal nor the State organisations are binding on their respective parliamentary wings.

Until the early 1980s, the Liberal Party tended to be more flexible than the ALP in its approach to politics. It held to some basic ideals and rejected socialism as a doctrine, but generally preferred to adapt its policies to the changing needs and wishes of the community. Since the election of the pragmatic, consensus-seeking and relatively conservative Hawke Labor Government, the Liberals have become more ideological and radical. That is to say, they are trying to define and win support for a more distinctive philosophy based on the values of individualism, personal independence, initiative and achievement, tolerance and fair play, and a lifestyle unfettered by government interference. This signals a move to the Right from the middle ground of Australian politics which always recognised that government has an important role in helping people, protecting their interests and welfare, providing community services and promoting a more egalitarian society.

According to a Liberal Party committee of review in 1983, the party is *for*: individual freedom and choice; support for and strengthening of the family; encouragement of enterprise, effort and excellence; appropriate reward for effort; economic growth through competitive private enterprise; protection and support for the weak; constitutional monarchy; parliamentary government and the rule of law; true Federalism and decentralisation of government; patriotism; and a strong, outward-looking Australia playing its full part in the region and the world. The Liberal Party is *against*: big, interventionist government; centralism and the 'Canberra knows best' approach; policies that discourage self-sufficiency, incentive and enterprise; and undue influence by powerful interest groups.

The Liberal Party is not divided into formal factions like the Labor Party, but it does have loose groupings of members based on differences of interpretation, emphasis and support for rival personalities. A distinction has long been made between the 'small "*l*" liberals' who, in the tradition of Alfred Deakin, tend to be more progressive, permissive and welfare-oriented, and the conservatives who have put a stronger emphasis on law and order, resistance to social change, and a tough-minded attitude in defence and foreign affairs. A new distinction in economic and industrial policy is between the 'wets', who believe in a fair degree of government intervention and regulation in the community interest, and the 'dries' or economic rationalists, who want to reduce the scope of government in economic affairs in favour of individual respons-ibility, free competition and market forces. Since the defeat of the Fraser Government in 1983, and especially under the leadership of John Howard and later John Hewson, the Liberals have emphasised the goals of privatisation (selling selected government enterprises to business interests), deregulation (fewer controls over industry, commerce and labour), phasing out of tariff protection for Australian manufacturers to promote competition, stronger support for development of Australian resources, and small government (fewer government responsibilities, a smaller public service and less government borrowing and spending). This, they believe, would stimulate economic growth and job creation, and make Australia more competitive in world trade. In 1991 the party announced a 'Fightback Program' with an emphasis on far-reaching reforms to taxation and industrial relations. The coalition parties' failure to win the Federal election in March 1993 is likely to prompt the Liberals to rethink and modify some of their policies to make them more attractive to a majority of voters. It has also led to continuing tensions over the party's leadership.

THE NATIONAL PARTY

The Country Party, as it was called for more than fifty years, was organised by farmers' and settlers' associations towards the end of the First World War. Many farmers and graziers were dissatisfied with the wartime schemes for the bulk marketing of primary products. Like the trade union movement some thirty years earlier, they turned to politics to protect and promote their interests.

The party grew quickly in strength and influence. After the Federal elections of 1922, the main non-Labor Party (then called Nationalists)

The Federal Opposition and Liberal Party Leader, Dr John Hewson, addresses an election rally during the 1993 campaign.

found itself unable to govern without Country Party support. The Country Party agreed to join a composite Government on certain conditions, including the right to veto Cabinet decisions. Since then, the main non-Labor party in Canberra has only twice governed alone, in 1932–34 and 1939–40. At other times, the Country Party has been the minority partner in non-Labor Governments or Oppositions, always insisting on a decisive say, at least on matters affecting country dwellers and rural problems.

To broaden its appeal, especially in country towns, the party has changed its name twice in the past twenty years. In 1975, the Federal party adopted the name National Country Party, which was also favoured in some States, while other States preferred the name National Party. In 1982, National Party became the name throughout Australia.

The National Party is strongest in Queensland, New South Wales and Victoria. Its concentration in country areas has enabled it to return a relatively high proportion of members to Parliament. The party has thus been able to exert an influence in politics far greater than its electoral support would indicate. In Queensland, it was able to govern alone or lead a coalition Government with the Liberals for thirty-two years until 1989. In New South Wales, it has been a partner in every non-Labor Government since 1927. In Victoria, the Country Party often held the balance of power until 1955, and at times ruled as a minority Government with Labor support. Since then, as in Western Australia, it has shrunk in parliamentary numbers and influence. In South Australia, the Country Party merged with the Liberal Party in 1933, but the National Party has revived, with limited success, as a separate party. In the Northern Territory, a coalition merger led to the formation of a combined Country Liberal Party.

Although the Labor and Liberal parties each attract more votes nationally, the National Party boasts a larger individual membership: about 140 000 in 1400 branches around Australia. As with the Liberal Party, the National Party in each State is autonomous, with its own constitution, rules and policies. The State parties are affiliated to the party's Federal organisation.

At State level, the party generally consists of local branches and electorate councils, an annual conference of branch and council delegates, a central council and a smaller management committee, executive council or State executive. Except in Queensland, conferences may set the general lines of party policy but cannot bind members to specific measures. In Queensland, however, State members of Parliament are required to abide by party policy. In Victoria, the State central council has the sole right to decide whether the party shall join a coalition Government.

The National Party's Federal organisation was restructured in 1988.

The supreme governing body is the Federal council, which consists of about seventy-seven members including all members of the Federal parliamentary party, delegates from all affiliated State parties, and representatives of the Women's Council and the Young National Party. Representatives of the Country–Liberal Party in the Northern Territory may attend as observers but have no voting rights. The Federal council meets at least once a year. The day-to-day management of the party is in the hands of a Federal Management Committee of fifteen members, comprising the president, treasurer and secretary, and representatives of the State parties, Federal parliamentary party, Federal Women's Council and Young National Party. There is also a Federal secretariat in Canberra.

The party's new constitution adopted in 1988 also provides for a Federal conference of up to 300 delegates (mostly branch members) to meet at least once during every Federal Parliament or every three years. It is the top policy-making body. The Federal parliamentary party is required, as far as possible, to implement party policy, but decisions of the Federal council or conference are not binding on its members.

The National Party not only represents country economic interests but also expresses rural and small town social values. In trying to defend and advance the financial well-being of the man (and woman) on the land, the party has often been opportunist, pragmatic and ruthless. At times it has allied itself with the Labor Party when it saw advantage in so doing; more often, it has pressed the Liberal Party, or its predecessors, for concessions, or formed political alliances with manufacturing and mining interests. In reflecting the moral values of its rural supporters, the party takes on an ideological tinge. It tends to be politically and socially conservative, expressing loyalty to God, Queen and country, opposing republicanism, extolling the virtues of family life and small communities, and deploring the social problems and moral permissiveness that many country people associate with the big cities.

In its early days, the party fought for the establishment of marketing boards (controlled by producers) and guaranteed prices for most major primary products except wool. Although it is opposed to what it calls socialism, the party has traditionally favoured government aid and concessions to help farmers and country dwellers—for example, cheap transport, roads, irrigation, water supply and electricity; low interest rates; and more schools and hospitals in the country. It believes that more people should be encouraged to live in the country, and favours assistance to manufacturers to set up industries in country towns. It tends to be highly critical of trade union demands for higher wages and shorter hours which would increase farmers' costs. The National Party strongly believes in federalism and the decentralisation of political power.

Although the National Party claims to be national in its policies, it is basically sectional and regional. Herein lies both its strength and weakness. Because of its concentration in rural areas and on rural affairs, it has long been a powerful and stable influence in Australian politics. However, with fewer people remaining on the land, small towns lagging in population growth and provincial centres becoming more urbanised, the party's electoral base is declining and its long-term future is in doubt, except perhaps in Queensland.

Under the leadership of Sir John McEwen (1958–71), the party made friends with city manufacturers by pressing for a high tariff protection policy in return for support for rural subsidies. When the Whitlam Labor Government (1972–75) began to reduce tariffs and rural subsidies, the party sought the support of mining and oil exploration companies opposed to Labor's minerals and energy policies. More recently, especially in Victoria, the National Party has tried to present itself as a champion of small business, claiming that the Liberals represented the interests of big business and Labor was too closely allied with powerful unions.

In the mid-1980s, partly under the influence of the newly formed National Farmers' Federation, some younger members of the National Party began to favour a change of economic direction. Like the 'economic rationalists' of the Liberal Party, they suggested that the interests of farmers would be best served by progressively exposing all Australian industries to free market forces rather than protecting them by regulation, tariffs and subsidies. Trade unions, they urged, should lose some of their legal privileges and the centralised wage-fixing system should be dismantled. The overall aim should be to make Australia internationally more competitive. In recent years, the National Party's intimate Federal coalition with the Liberal Party has resulted in a closer alignment of their policies in this new direction, despite some dissent from among older rank and file members of the party.

In Queensland, the National Party prospered over most of the twenty-one year leadership of Sir Joh Bjelke-Petersen from 1969 to 1987. The success of his Government—ruling in its own right or with the Liberals as junior coalition partners—was partly due to the electoral system (see Chapter 6) and the internal problems of the other parties. But the veteran Premier also won wide support by exploiting State and local loyalties and prejudices (against Canberra, the southern States, the big cities, 'socialism' and 'permissiveness') and by emphasising economic development and law and order (at the expense, according to his critics, of environmental concerns, civil liberties and the rights of trade unions and Aboriginal people). His rather autocratic rule became discredited by the conspicuous failure of his attempt to enter Federal politics as head of a new conservative grouping and by the disclosures of the Fitzgerald Royal Commission of ingrained police corruption and political favours to political cronies. His party replaced him as Premier in 1987 and was itself decisively defeated by a reformist Labor Government in 1989.

The National Party has, however, remained the dominant non-Labor party in the Queensland Parliament, and did have some success before its downfall in winning outer metropolitan seats as an alternative to the Liberal Party. It now seems unlikely to expand either in Queensland or in other States. There, and federally, the party may in future have to choose between trying to keep its separate identity in the face of dwindling support, or seeking closer links, and perhaps eventual amalgamation, with the Liberal Party.

THE AUSTRALIAN DEMOCRATS

From time to time, small political parties emerge, either dedicated to a particular cause (such as nuclear disarmament) or offering a broad alternative to the established parties. Unless they have a strong regional base, like the National Party, they have little chance of winning seats in houses of Parliament with single-member electorates. However, they may gain places in the Senate and State upper Houses where the voting system is by proportional representation (as explained in Chapter 6).

The Australian Democrats, a broadly based party formed in 1975, attracted a remarkable popular response when it won eleven per cent of the national vote for the Senate in the 1977 election (sixteen per cent in Victoria). Led by a former Liberal Member of Parliament, Don Chipp, the new party offered itself as a 'third force' between the Liberal–NCP coalition on the right and the Labor Party on the left. Mr Chipp and a New South Wales colleague were elected to the Senate, but the party's immediate aim of gaining the balance of power there was not realised until July 1981, when the number of Democrat senators rose to five. With the Labor Opposition and an Independent senator, the Democrats were able to block a number of Government measures. In December 1984, the number of Democrat senators increased to seven, a strength the party seems unlikely to maintain in future elections. In 1985, the party also had one member in the New South Wales Legislative Council and two in the South Australian Legislative Council.

The Australian Democrats developed from two earlier parties, the Australia Party and the South Australian New Liberal Reform Movement. The Australia Party began as the Liberal Reform Group which contested the 1966 Federal election largely as a protest against

Australia's involvement in the Vietnam War. In 1967 its name changed to the Australian Reform Movement and in 1969 it became the Australia Party. Its nationalistic and libertarian policies were closer to those of the ALP than the Liberal Party, and its electoral preferences helped Labor win some seats in the 1972 election. After the 1975 election, the Australia Party seemed set to decline in membership and influence. The New Liberal Movement—a remnant of a split in the South Australian Liberal Party—was also waning. The two groups found a common basis for a new political movement in the widespread public discontent and disillusionment with both the ALP and Liberal–NCP coalition after 1975— and they found a popular leader in Don Chipp. Most members of the Australia Party and New Liberal Movement rallied to the new movement under the name of Australian Democrats, which also attracted new members from the major parties and from people not previously active in politics.

In his 1977 election campaign, Mr Chipp called for a return to the political virtues of 'honesty, tolerance and compassion' as opposed to the politics of 'cynicism, opportunism and confrontation'. He urged people to support his party as an independent, incorruptible, middle-of-the-road 'watchdog' in the Senate. He promised that it would not join either of the major parties in a coalition or in blocking Supply to bring down a Government.

In structure, the Australian Democrats claim to be more democratic than the other parties, insisting that all members should take part in formulating and approving its policies, and electing its leaders. The party has emphasised the importance of individual liberty, social justice and constitutional reform, and advocated policies to reduce unemployment and create jobs, improve industrial relations and social welfare, and help small business, farmers and people on fixed incomes. In the past ten years it has moved to the Left of the Labor Party in some ways, competing for votes with the short-lived Nuclear Disarmament Party and the newer Green parties based on conservation and environmental issues. In the 1993 election campaign it offered itself as an alternative to the hard 'economic rationalist' policies of the major parties, opposing the rapid scaling down of tariff protection for Australian manufacturers, the dismantling of the centralised arbitration system and the goods and services tax proposed by the coalition.

The Australian Democrats have exerted an important influence on Australian politics in three respects. First, by holding themselves out as a party of alternative ideas and ideals, they have attracted votes from people dissatisfied with the major parties. Second, by directing their preferences in elections (see Chapter 6), they have been able, like the Democratic Labor Party in earlier years, to influence the outcome of election results in some seats. Whereas DLP preferences helped to keep the conservative parties in Parliament for many years federally and in Victoria, the Democrat preferences have tended to favour Labor by an estimated fifty-five to seventy per cent. And third, by holding the balance of power in the Senate, they have been able to force the Government to modify some legislation to meet their wishes as the price of their support, or throw their weight behind the Opposition to block some other legislation or tax changes to which they objected.

The future of the Australian Democrats depends partly on their internal cohesion—they were weakened in the 1993 Federal election campaign by divisions over their leadership—and partly on external factors. One such factor is the electoral system. They have little chance of winning single-member electorates in Federal or State lower Houses, and their continuing strength in the Senate depends on how much of the alternative or protest vote they can attract. Here they are being challenged by the emergent Greens, with whom they may have to merge and ally themselves to remain an effective 'third force' in political life.

SINGLE-ISSUE PARTIES

Single-issue political parties may sometimes capture the imagination— and votes—of a great many people. Some are more durable and successful than others. For example, the Reverend Fred Nile, national coordinator of the Festival of Light, has been able to hold a seat in the NSW Legislative Council since 1981, and so has his wife Elaine since 1988. As representatives of the Call to Australia Group, their platform is based on support for conservative Christian morals and opposition to abortion, prostitution, homosexuality and sexual permissiveness.

THE GREENS

While the Australian Democrats have an established national organ-isation and broad spectrum of policies, the Greens are more loosely allied and have a narrower focus. Inspired by similar parties in Europe, they have evolved from the conservationist and environmentalist movement and the Nuclear Disarmament Party (NDP) of the mid-1980s.

The NDP was founded in 1984 by a group of academics, writers and others who were disillusioned with the Hawke Government's unwilling-ness to implement and toughen the ALP's platform on the peaceful and military uses of nuclear energy. The new party called for the banning of mining and export of Australian uranium, the exclusion of nuclear weapons from Australian soil, waters and airspace, the removal of American joint defence facilities from Australia, and international nuclear disarmament. The NDP won nearly seven per cent of the vote for the Senate in the 1984 election, returning one Senator, Ms Jo Vallentine, for Western Australia. The party was soon split by international disagreements and waned in popular support. Ms Vallentine took her Senate seat as an Independent and successfully contested the 1990 election as a Greens candidate. She resigned in 1992 but in 1993 two other WA Greens were elected to the Senate.

Meanwhile, the Greens have formed a national organisation covering several States under the leadership of Dr Bob Brown, who resigned from the Tasmanian Parliament in an unsuccessful attempt to win a House of Representatives seat in 1993. The Tasmanian Greens were an offshoot from the Tasmanian Wilderness Society which successfully opposed the building of a dam for hydro-electricity on the Franklin River in 1983. The Greens, who also opposed logging of native forests for the development of wood-chipping and paper pulp mills, won two seats in the Tasmanian Parliament in 1986 and, with eighteen per cent of the vote, five seats in 1989. Their success helped to bring down the Liberal State Government and they entered into a unique power-sharing alliance with the incoming Labor Government. This broke down after fifteen months, but their qualified support enabled Labor to rule as a minority Government until early 1992, when the Liberals were returned to power with a clear majority over Labor and three remaining Green Independents.

The strength of the Green movement significantly influenced ALP policies and boosted Labor's vote in the 1990 Federal election, but less so in the 1993 election, when the Keating Government was more concerned with hard economic issues. The future of the Greens as a political force will depend on the degree to which voters (and the major parties) give priority to environmental over economic issues. They might in future revert to becoming a pressure group rather than a party with parliamentary representatives, or merge with the Australian Democrats.

THE DEMOCRATIC LABOR PARTY

The Democratic Labor Party developed after the third great split in the ALP and played an influential role in Australian politics for nearly twenty years. In the early 1950s, strongly anti-communist ALP members formed 'industrial groups' to fight communist leadership and influence in a number of trade unions affiliated with the Labor Party. In October 1954, the Federal Labor leader, Dr H.V. Evatt, made a dramatic statement declaring that the industrial groups were being directed by a secret organisation of Catholic laymen known as 'the Movement' led by Mr B.A. Santamaria. He accused it of trying, like the communists, to control the ALP itself.

The Federal executive supported Dr Evatt and brought about the dissolution of the industrial groups in the unions. In the wake of the conflict, many parliamentary, executive and ordinary members of the ALP broke away or were expelled, and formed rival parties which subsequently united under the title of Democratic Labor Party. The DLP's only sustained parliamentary success was to hold the balance of power in the Senate from 1967 to 1974. But more importantly, by persuading many voters to give their second preferences in elections to the Liberal or Country Parties, the DLP prevented the Labor Party from coming to power in Canberra until 1972. It also helped to keep anti-Labor Governments in office in Victoria and Queensland for many years. After 1974, the party rapidly declined in political influence and public support. Its strong anti-communism, 'anti-permissiveness' stance and its heavy emphasis on defence and law and order had lost much of their electoral appeal, the ALP had regained the confidence of many voters, and the conservative parties no longer needed DLP support.

THE COMMUNIST PARTIES AND EXTREME LEFT

Founded in Australia in 1920, the Communist Party was for seventy years a small but active, influential and widely feared party dedicated to the overthrow of the capitalist system and class structure, and its replacement by a socialist society. Increasingly split and diminished in the 1970s and 1980s, it disbanded in 1990, leaving the extreme Left of politics to a number of very small groups with hardly any electoral support.

Although the Communist Party contested many Federal and State elections in the past, it only ever held one seat, for a few years in the Queensland Parliament. Its greatest success was to capture important positions in key trade unions. Mainly through these unions, it sought to influence the policy of the ALP, while competing with the ALP for working-class support. Fears of communist influence in the Labor movement led to the 1954 split in the ALP and the formation of the anti-communist Democratic Labor Party. From the 1950s Communists were also active, as their ideological successors still try to be, in organisations opposed to war, nuclear arms and uranium mining, and in the civil rights, anti-racism, anti-apartheid, Aboriginal land rights, environmentalist and feminist movements.

Decline and division increasingly sapped the viability of the Communist Party since the mid-1950s, as a result of relative economic prosperity in Australia and such overseas developments as the denunciation of the Stalin dictatorship by the Soviet leader, Mr Khrushchev, in 1956, the Soviet invasions of Hungary (1956) and Czechoslovakia (1968) and the growing hostility between the Soviet Union and China. In the early 1980s, there were three separate parties. They were the Communist Party of Australia, formerly influenced by Russian Communism but by now increasingly independent; the Communist Party of Australia (Marxist-Leninist), which drew inspiration from Chinese Communism; and the Socialist Party of Australia, which was regarded as pro-Moscow. The CPA was further split when most of its Victorian executive broke away to form the Socialist Forum, bringing together a wider range of far-Left opinion.

The collapse of the ruling Communist parties in the disintegrating Soviet Union and its allied countries of Eastern Europe in 1990 ended the formal existence of the Communist parties in Australia. By the early 1990s major elements of the non-Labor Left had regrouped as the New Left Party and the small Socialist Workers Party changed its name to the Democratic Socialist Party. There were still also some other minor radical and revolutionary Left groups. Some former Communist union leaders, such as John Halfpenny in Victoria, were readmitted to the ALP.

Pressure Groups

Like political parties, pressure groups exist to promote causes or protect interests; unlike parties, they do not seek power to govern. Instead, they hope to influence Governments, and in so doing, play an important role in formulating demands, expressing attitudes and making claims. They may do so openly, through submissions, petitions, public meetings and press statements, or privately, by 'lobbying' Ministers, Members of Parliament or officials. Pressure groups operate at both Federal and State levels, even at local levels. Some maintain permanent secretariats in

Canberra. Sometimes Government will consult with interest groups before deciding policy or drafting legislation. Governments are often under conflicting pressures, for and against particular courses of action.

Australia has an enormous number and astonishing variety of pressure or interest groups, some more persuasive than others. The most influential and persistent groups represent organised labour, commerce, industry, mining and farming interests. Since 1983 the Australian Council of Trade Unions (ACTU) has had a substantial influence on wages, prices and tax policy through its special relationship and Accord with the Hawke and Keating Labor Governments. More than 2 500 000 Australians, or about forty per cent of all employees, are members of trade unions. In the late 1980s, there were more than 300 unions, most of them affiliated with the ACTU and/or State trades and labour councils. A Government and ACTU-sponsored program of amalgamations aims to reduce the number to about twenty powerful unions, each with tens to hundreds of thousands of members.

The interests of employers are represented nationally by the Australian Chamber of Commerce and Industry (ACCI), formed in 1992 by a merger of the Confederation of Australian Industry and the Australian Chamber of Commerce. It represents about 300 000 businesses. Also important is the Business Council of Australia (BCA) founded in 1983 by the chief executives of some of Australia's biggest companies. The peak organisation of primary producers is now the National Farmers' Federation, representing a number of State and Northern Territory farming organisations and commodity councils.

Among other numerous special-interest groups are organisations representing ex-servicemen and women, pensioners, consumers, the professions, churches, Aboriginal people, ethnic communities, motorists, conservationists, women's interests, students, the unemployed, and independent schools. There are also well-established lobbies speaking up for social welfare, civil liberties, sport and the arts.

Most of the pressure groups mentioned so far represent sectional but continuing interests. In recent years there has also been a growth in associations aiming to promote particular causes and to influence public opinion as well as governments directly. Their causes are often controversial and their tactics range from the secretive to the demonstrative. A long-established behind-the-scenes political group is the National Civic Council which developed, like the DLP, from a movement of Catholic laypeople to counter communist influence in the trade unions, and promote self-reliance in national defence and support for Christian values. Other groups are more radical and transitory. They may resort to demonstrations, protest marches and sit-ins. A number of militant groups were formed in the late 1960s to oppose Australia's participation in the

Vietnam War and conscription for military service. Others, opposed to racial discrimination, took action against visits by sporting teams from South Africa. There are active groups for and against abortion law reform, and for women's and homosexual 'liberation'. Concern for the natural environment has provoked a number of groups, some with broad and long-term aims, and others with specific goals, such as to prevent the mining of uranium, protection of native and rain forests or the flooding of wild rivers in south-west Tasmania. At the local level, groups of residents may form to oppose road projects or building developments.

A fairly recent development in Canberra is the emergence of professional lobbyists who, for a fee, will try to influence or inform Governments, Members of Parliament or departments for clients. Sometimes a pressure group will put forward candidates in elections: the Council for the Defence of Government Schools, which is opposed to State aid for church schools, has (unsuccessfully) contested elections. But the Right to Life movement has claimed success in Victoria in bringing about the defeat of parliamentary candidates not sufficiently in sympathy with its firm opposition to abortion. Some pressure groups develop into political parties, like the Greens, with members in Parliament.

For further thought

- How much discipline should parties exert over their parliamentary members in the interests of stable Government or effective Opposition?
- Should Members of Parliament who disagree with their party's policy on a particular subject accept the majority decision and vote with their colleagues, or should they be free to speak and vote in Parliament according to their conscience?
- Critics have described the Labor Party as being too much under the control of the trade union movement, and the Liberal Party as being too closely associated with business. How true are their allegations?
- Is socialism relevant to the economic and social problems of present-day Australia? How far has the Labor Party departed from its socialist principles of the past?
- What useful purpose, if any, do minority parties serve in the Australian parliamentary system? Should a third party, if it holds the balance of power in an upper House, use its position to try to impose its will on a Government?
- What future do you see for the Australian Democrats and the Greens?
- Many young people have shown impatience with the parliamentary process and preferred to demonstrate in the streets. In what circumstances, if any, do you regard such direct action as being justified?

CHAPTER

6

ELECTIONS

In a parliamentary democracy such as ours, elections are the means by which the people can regularly control their Government. The people have no direct part in the making or carrying out of laws, but they have the right, every so often, to elect the men and women they want to represent them in Parliament, where laws are made and Governments are formed.

It may be argued that the people do not really choose their parliamentary representatives, as almost all of them are 'preselected' by political parties. Even so, voters have a degree of choice: they may vote for a candidate of this party or of that party, knowing that the party with a majority of members elected to the lower House of Parliament will form the Government.

In this way, not only individual Members of Parliament but also Governments are called to account for their policies and actions. The people, as electors, can review the records of their representatives, and by their votes, pass judgement. A popular Government will probably be returned to power, and an unpopular one defeated and replaced.

Democratic elections require a number of essential conditions. The foremost—which we take for granted in Australia—is the right of political parties and individual citizens to stand and campaign for election in opposition to the Government in power. In some countries, 'elections' are a sham, as voters have no real choice. They have no opportunity to vote for an alternative Government because no genuine Opposition is tolerated.

If we assume this right to contest political office freely, there are still some basic rules for the conduct of democratic elections.

The first is *universal suffrage*: the principle that every adult citizen should be entitled to vote. This now applies to elections for all Australian Parliaments. All Australian citizens aged eighteen or more, living in Australia, have the right and responsibility to enrol and vote at Commonwealth elections and referendums.

Formerly, British subjects who were not Australian citizens were also entitled to vote. They may continue to do so only if they were already on the electoral roll on 25 January 1984, when the law was changed. Seventeen-year-olds may enrol for Federal elections but not vote unless they have turned eighteen by polling day.

A person must have lived in an electorate for a month before enrolment, but special arrangements are made for people with no fixed address. Anyone who is of unsound mind, convicted of treason or serving a sentence for an offence punishable by imprisonment for five years or longer, is disqualified.

Qualifications for State elections are similar, but may vary in detail. Most States have a joint electoral roll with the Commonwealth. Aboriginal people were given the right to vote by Federal law in 1962 and in all States by 1965. More recently, the minimum voting age was reduced from twenty-one to eighteen for Federal and all State elections, beginning in Western Australia in 1971. As late as 1973 in South Australia, voters for some Legislative Councils had to have property or war service qualifications.

The second requirement for democratic elections is that the *qualifications* for Members of Parliament should not be too restrictive. A candidate for the Senate or House of Representatives must be at least eighteen years old, an Australian citizen, and an elector or qualified to be an elector. No one may nominate for more than one seat at a time. A

member of one House may not be chosen for the other unless he or she first resigns. Nor may a member of a State parliament or Territory Assembly. Constitutional disqualifications include allegiance to a foreign power, being under or subject to sentence for a crime punishable by imprisonment for a year or more, being bankrupt, holding office of profit under the Crown (with certain exceptions) or having any financial interest in agreement with the Government except as a member of a company of more than twenty-five shareholders. Qualifications for members of State legislatures are broadly similar but may differ in detail.

The third essential for democratic elections is that they be *held at regular and reasonable intervals*. If there were no regular elections, Governments could become lazy or extravagant or dictatorial. Elections should be often enough to keep Governments in touch with public opinion, but not so frequently that Governments are unable to carry out their work effectively.

Under the Federal Constitution, elections for the House of Representatives must be held at least every three years. The life of a Parliament is limited, but not fixed. Elections may be held before the end of the normal term if the Prime Minister for some serious reason, such as the defeat of vital legislation or a vote of no-confidence, or because it is felt that it would be politically advantageous to do so, recommends to the Governor-General that the lower House should be dissolved.

Elections for the Queensland Parliament must also be held within three years. New South Wales, Victoria and Western Australia have extended the maximum terms of their lower Houses from three years to four, while Tasmania in 1976 reduced its House of Assembly term from five years to four. South Australia's Legislative Assembly now has a minimum term of three years and a maximum of four years. Members of all State upper Houses except Western Australia's are elected for longer terms, and not all retire at the same time. This provides continuity in what are supposed to be chambers of review.

Senators representing the States are also normally elected for six years, and half of them retire every three years. Their term of service begins on 1 July following the election. In the case of a double dissolution, all Senators must face election. Half of the State Senators—those with the most votes—will then serve for six years, and the rest for three years. Terms of service after a double dissolution are counted from 1 July preceding the election. Senators from the Northern Territory and Australian Capital Territory face re-election every time there is an election for the House of Representatives.

Members of the New South Wales Legislative Council serve three terms of the Legislative Assembly (up to twelve years) but a third retire at each election. Legislative Councillors in Victoria and South Australia now serve for two lower House terms (up to eight years), half retiring at each election. In Tasmania, the term is also for six years, but an election is held every year for three (sometimes four) of the members. Since 1987, Western Australian members of the Legislative Council are elected for up to four years, the same period as their Lower House colleagues.

The fourth requirement of democratic elections is that they be *conducted honestly and by secret ballot*. Australia led the world in adopting the secret ballot, which was first used in Victorian elections in 1856. In America, the secret ballot is still often called the 'Australian ballot'. Each voter is given an unmarked ballot paper on which are printed the names of the candidates and a blank space beside each name. On ballot papers for Federal and most State elections, candidates are now identified by their party affiliations. Voters fill in the paper in private, fold it and drop it into a sealed box, so that no one knows how they voted. The secrecy is to ensure that every elector can vote as they choose, without fear of reprisal.

Not only is voting secret, but also the whole procedure is honest. Australian electors can be sure that their vote will be counted, that it will go to the candidate for whom they voted, and that only genuine votes will be included in the count. Elections are conducted by independent officials under strict regulations, and votes are counted under the scrutiny of the candidates' representatives.

The fifth requirement is summed up in the phrase *one vote, one value*. The principle of 'one person, one vote'—that every adult citizen should

have one vote, and one vote only—has long been adopted. The principle of one vote, one value, has taken longer to be accepted, and even now it is not fully implemented in some States.

For the House of Representatives, the Commonwealth Constitution provides that each State shall be divided into electorates (also called constituencies), each with about the same number of electors. The number is found by dividing the number of electorates in a State by the number of members to be elected for that State. A variation of ten per cent either way is permitted, to allow for faster growth in some areas over others. In the past, however, this variation, formerly twenty per cent, was used to allot fewer voters to country areas. Each electorate returns one member to the House of Representatives. In 1990, the Federal electorates averaged about 72 000 voters each. As every State is to have at least five members, the Tasmanian electorates have fewer electors. Tasmania uses these constituencies for its House of Assembly elections, returning seven members from each electorate.

For the Tasmanian upper House, and still to a limited extent in Queensland and Western Australia, many more voters are enrolled for city than for rural electorates. This gives the country vote added value and country people proportionately more representation in Parliament. This has been justified in two ways:

1 that it is fair compensation for the difficulties of distance and scattered population, and
2 that rural areas and industries are 'the backbone of the country' and deserve protection against domination by the big cities.

Critics reply that:

1 better communications have lessened the disability of distance and that extra travel allowances and secretarial help for country Members of Parliament could lessen it further, and
2 that rural industries are declining in relative importance and in any case Members of Parliament are supposed to represent people, not acres or industries.

Politically, the deliberate inequality in favour of rural areas gave a big advantage until the late 1980s to the National Party in Queensland and the Liberal Party in Western Australia, where they used their majorities to resist reform. In Tasmania, the Legislative Council is still dominated by conservative 'Independents' who have traditionally remained aloof from formal party affiliation.

However, sweeping reform has been achieved in Queensland and Western Australia, where a vote in the outback might have been worth three to four times as much as a vote in the city. In Queensland since

1991, all but five of the eighty-nine electorates now have an equal number of voters (subject to a permissible ten per cent variation). Five rural districts of more than 100 000 square kilometres are allowed a smaller quota of voters. In Western Australia, the disparities between metropolitan, farming and outback electorates have been greatly reduced since 1987.

For the Senate, each State is also treated as a single electorate. Each returns twelve Senators, regardless of population differences. Thus more than 3 600 000 electors of New South Wales are represented by twelve Senators, and so is Tasmania with scarcely 300 000 voters. There has been no great objection to this inequality, because of the idea of the Senate as a *States' House* and because no major political party is at a disadvantage as a result.

Victoria's Legislative Council has twenty-two electorates (called provinces) with two members each. One member is returned at one election and the other at the next. Western Australia's Legislative Council now has six regions: the south-west and three metropolitan regions each return seven members every election, and the agricultural and mining–pastoral regions each return five. Tasmania's upper House has nine single-member provinces. The NSW and South Australian Legislative Councils are elected by proportional representation with each State as a single electorate.

COMPULSORY VOTING

Australia is unusual among English-speaking countries in having adopted compulsory enrolment of voters and compulsory voting. This was first introduced in Queensland in 1915 and by the Commonwealth in 1924. Now it applies to all Australian elections except those for the South Australian upper House. Penalties for not voting are small—a fine of up to $50 in Federal elections.

Voting, once regarded as a hard-won right, is now a positive duty. For many, unfortunately, it is a tiresome task. Those who brought about compulsory voting hoped that it would make people more interested in political affairs, but it is doubtful whether it has had this effect. In the last Federal election before the introduction of compulsory voting, only fifty-nine per cent of eligible electors voted. Now between ninety and ninety-six per cent vote. The main effect of compulsory voting has been to make things easier for political parties, who no longer have to spend time and money in trying to persuade people to enrol and vote at all.

BY-ELECTIONS

When a member of Parliament dies or resigns between elections, a by-election is usually held to fill the vacancy. In the Tasmanian House of Assembly, however, the candidate who came second in the last election normally becomes the new member.

The Senate and the Legislative Councils of New South Wales and South Australia have different methods of filling a casual vacancy. The new Senator is elected by a joint sitting of both Houses of Parliament in the State where the vacancy occurs. If the Houses are not sitting, then the State Government appoints a Senator until the Houses do sit.

For many years it was a convention that a 'casual' Senator would be picked from the same party as that of his or her predecessor. But in two controversial appointments in 1975, the New South Wales and Queensland Governments nominated non-Labor Senators to replace a Labor Senator who resigned to become a High Court judge, and another who died. As a result of a referendum in 1977, a casual Senate vacancy now must be filled, if possible, by a person of the same party. The new Senator holds the seat for the remainder of the predecessor's term.

New South Wales has adopted a similar system to fill casual vacancies in its Legislative Council. A casual vacancy in the South Australian upper House is filled by a joint sitting of both Houses.

REDISTRIBUTION

As populations increase and some areas grow more quickly than others, it becomes necessary after some years to alter the boundaries of electorates to provide for more members of Parliament or to even out the number of voters in each electorate. This has to be done regularly, and without political interference or delay, if the system is to be fair and honest. The appointment of a permanent, independent Australian Electoral Commission has ensured this for Federal elections. The commission is responsible not only for the conduct of Federal elections and referendums but also for redistributions of electoral boundaries. A redistribution is required within a State whenever population changes mean that it should have more (or fewer) members in the House of Representatives, or if a third of the electorates in the State or one of the Australian Capital Territory electorates varies from the average enrolment by more than ten per cent, or if seven years have passed since the last redistribution.

In redrawing boundaries, the commission takes into account the community of economic, social and regional interests, means of communication and travel, population trends, physical features and area, and existing boundaries. The commission's redistribution committees will invite suggestions and hear objections, but decisions are final, and not subject to legal challenge or parliamentary approval. New South Wales, Victoria and South Australia now have broadly similar systems.

The terms *gerrymander* and *malapportionment* are sometimes used by those who believe that electoral boundaries have been deliberately and unfairly distorted. Malapportionment (or maldistribution) is the more accurate term for electoral inequalities which are:

1 intentionally created by the zoning of electorates, such as to give country votes relatively more value than city votes, or
2 allowed to develop by the failure of Governments to hold regular and reasonably frequent redistributions to take account of population movements.

Where regular redistributions are not required by law, or not left to independent electoral commissions, Parliaments have at times been tempted to delay making electoral adjustments that could mean that some Members of Parliament might lose their seats or that one or other party would be disadvantaged.

The term *gerrymander* comes from the name of an unscrupulous American politician, Governor Elbridge Gerry of Massachusetts, who, in 1812, had the electoral map of his State redrawn to his advantage, the shape of one district resembling a salamander. So strictly speaking, a gerrymander means arranging electoral boundaries to maximise the vote for one party and disadvantage its opponents.

Until recently, electoral boundaries in Queensland and Western Australia were grossly malapportioned. In Queensland and in some other States without independent electoral commissions, some electorates had also been gerrymandered to favour the ruling party.

Even under perfectly fair redistributions in a system of single-member electorates, one party or another may be at a disadvantage. In the past, this was usually the Labor Party, because its supporters tended to be more highly concentrated in industrial suburbs and towns. Thus Labor would often pile large and wasteful majorities in its safe seats while its opponents won more seats with narrower margins. This disparity has generally diminished with population changes, and in some States, the conservative parties may now require a slightly higher percentage of the total vote than Labor to win office.

ELECTION FUNDING

In May 1981, the Labor Government of New South Wales became the first in Australia to adopt the idea of providing public funds to political parties for their election campaigns. At the same time, it required public disclosure of election expenses and private gifts to campaign funds. In February 1984, the Federal Government introduced a similar public funding and disclosure scheme for Federal elections. The Federal arrangements are administered by the Australian Electoral Commission. To claim a share of the available funds, a political party, independent candidate or Senate group must first register with the commission and then win at least four per cent of the formal first preference votes at the relevant election. The rate of payment is adjusted every six months for inflation. In the 1990 Federal elections, the parties received about ninety cents for every House of Representatives vote and about forty-five cents for every Senate vote they won.

Payments may not be more than actually spent. All parties, candidates and groups, whether registered for public funding or not, must disclose their campaign spending. They must also report all donations of $1000 or more by an organisation and of $200 or more by an individual. Any donations of $200 or more to an individual candidate must also be reported.

The arguments for and against public funding have been based on democratic principles and on the balance of political advantage. Supporters of the idea argue that election campaigns have become increasingly expensive, especially with the greater use of television advertising. Without public funding, financially weaker and smaller parties find it difficult to match the campaign spending of parties with wealthier support. Public funding also reduces the dependence of political parties on secret or open gifts from business interests, trade unions and pressure groups who might expect favours in return. In short, it may be said that public funding makes for greater equality and honesty.

Opponents say that it is wrong for public funds to be used for partisan purposes, that private contributions are a legitimate measure of a party's popular support, and that dependency on public subsidies reduces a party's incentive to recruit members prepared to back their beliefs with money and work. Some critics also argue that a more sensible (and less expensive) approach would be to limit campaign spending, such as by banning or restricting television advertising, which can be highly misleading. In 1992 the Federal Labor Government tried to ban political advertising on radio and television during elections to keep campaign costs in check. However, the High Court ruled its legislation invalid as an unjustifiable restriction on freedom of expression.

The Labor Party and Australian Democrats are strongly in favour of public funding. The Liberal and National Parties have opposed the idea, but accepted a share of funds when schemes have been introduced. There have been similar divisions over disclosure of gifts and spending.

In the 1990 Federal election, registered parties, groups and candidates were entitled to nearly $13 million in public funding, according to the Australian Electoral Commission. They probably spent about twice that much.

SYSTEMS OF VOTING

The outcome of an election is influenced not only by the distribution of electoral boundaries but also, more basically, by the voting system used. Three systems have been used in Australia—simple majority voting, preferential voting and proportional representation—each of which can give differing results. Let us look at them one by one before discussing their respective merits and political effects.

SIMPLE MAJORITY VOTING

This system, which is used in Britain, is sometimes called 'first past the post'. People simply vote for one of the candidates standing in each electorate, and the one with the most votes wins. Queensland used this system from 1942 until 1963, when preferential voting was reintroduced.

Suppose there are three candidates, whom we shall call Black, White and Green, in an electorate of 10 000 voters. The election might give this result:

Black	3450
White	3350
Green	3200

Black would be elected, although 6550 of the 10 000 electors voted against Black.

PREFERENTIAL VOTING

This system, also known as the alternative vote, has been gradually adopted in Australia since 1919. Electors vote for the candidates in order of preference. They write the figure 1 in the square opposite the name of their preferred candidate, 2 beside their second choice, 3 beside their next choice, and so on down the list.

If one candidate receives an absolute majority—more votes than those of the other candidates together—that candidate is elected. But if no candidate has an absolute majority, the one with the fewest first preference votes is eliminated, and those votes are distributed among the remaining candidates according to his or her second preferences.

Let us suppose an election had the same result, on the first preferences, as the one in the previous example: Black, 3450; White, 3350; and Green, 3200. Green would be eliminated and those second preferences counted. Of these, 1700 might go to White and 1500 to Black. The result would then be:

Black   3450 + 1500 = 4950

White   3350 + 1700 = 5050

White would be the winner.

PROPORTIONAL REPRESENTATION

The aim of this system, also known as quota-preferential, is to give the various political parties representation in Parliament according to the proportion of votes their candidates win. Instead of single member electorates, it is necessary to have large electorates returning several members.

Proportional representation (PR) has been used for the Tasmanian House of Assembly since 1907 and the Senate since 1948. It has also been introduced for the New South Wales and South Australian Legislative Councils and the Australian Capital Territory Legislative Assembly. Proportional representation was adopted for Senate elections because preferential voting in the multi-member electorates (each State being one electorate) gave the most successful party representation out of all proportion to its electoral support.

Although proportional representation has its variations in Australia, the basic principles are the same. A candidate is elected when he or she wins a certain share of all the first preference votes cast. This share is known as the quota. It is found by dividing the number of candidates to be elected plus one into the total number of formal votes, and adding one to the result.

Tasmania uses the Hare-Clark method of proportional representation. A detailed description of this method is given in the Tasmanian Year Book.

In Senate elections, six members are elected for each State every three years. Under a new system first used in the 1984 elections, the Senate ballot paper for each State has two sections. On the lower section, as in the past, candidates' names are arranged in columns according to party, independents being grouped in the last column. People who wish to vote for individual candidates or the independents must place a consecutive number in every square, in any order they wish, to indicate their preferences.

Most people, however, vote for a party rather than for particular candidates. They can now do so quite simply on the new Senate ballot papers. Above each column of party candidates is a box, identified by the name of the party or group. All the voter need do is to write the figure 1 in the box for the party of their choice. No further preferences are required.

Lots are drawn for the position of each party on the ballot paper. The Liberal and National Parties nominate joint teams in some States.

The idea of requiring a single vote for a party rather than preferences for individual candidates was first adopted here by South Australia in 1973 for its Legislative Council elections. This system was abandoned in 1981 in favour of the dual method introduced for the Senate, except that preferences for individual candidates need be marked for no more than the number to be elected.

New South Wales has also adopted optional proportional representation, but without the option of a party block vote, for its Legislative Council. Voters have to mark preferences for ten candidates, but no more.

A candidate is elected when he or she wins a certain share of all the first preference votes cast. This share is known as the quota. It is found by dividing the number of candidates to be elected plus one into the total number of formal votes, and adding one to the result.

Suppose there are six candidates, with three to be elected, and a total of 10 000 votes have been cast. (In an actual Senate election, of course, there are far more candidates and votes.) The quota in our example is:

$$\frac{10\ 000}{3 + 1} + 1$$

$$\frac{10\ 000}{4} + 1$$

$$2500 + 1 = 2501$$

Any candidate who gains the quota of 2501 votes or more is elected.

When some candidates win more votes than the quota, their 'surplus' votes are transferred according to their second preferences, but each preference vote is worth only a fraction of a full vote. The 'transfer value fraction' is obtained by dividing the elected candidate's total surplus votes by his or her total preference votes.

All the first preference ballot papers of the elected candidates are

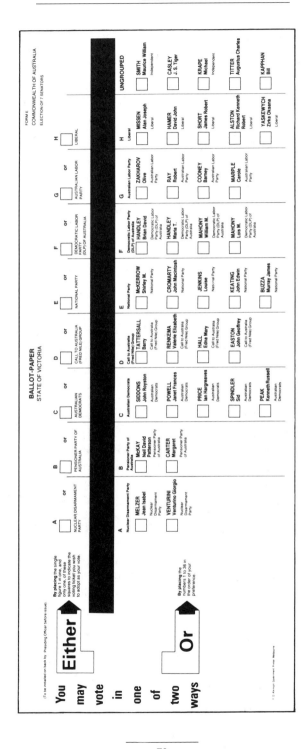

A Senate ballot paper. Note the option of voting for the party or for individual candidates.

sorted into separate parcels according to the second preferences shown on them. The total of each parcel is multiplied by the 'transfer value fraction'. The results are added to the appropriate candidate's original totals. As a candidate by this process gains enough preferences to reach the quota, then the candidate is elected. In turn, any surplus votes are passed on in this way.

If, after all the surplus votes have been distributed, the required number of candidates have not gained their quota, the candidate with the fewest votes is eliminated, and his or her preferences are distributed, each counting as a full vote. This process continues until the required number of members has been elected.

To go on with our example: the candidate and their first preference votes are:

Black	3500
Brown	3250
Gold	1500
Green	1000
Grey	500
White	250
Total	10 000

The quota, you will recall, is 2501. As Black and Brown have exceeded this figure, they are both elected. Black has 999 surplus votes, making the transfer value of Black's preferences 999/3500. Brown has 749 surplus votes, making the transfer value of Brown's preferences 749/3250.

Black's original 3500 votes are sorted according to second preferences, of which, let us say, 1750 go to White, 1000 to Grey and 750 to Green. These are multiplied by the transfer value fraction, 999/3500, to give the actual number of votes to be transferred: 500 to White, 285 to Grey and 214 to Green.

Brown's second preferences are allocated as follows: 1500 to Gold, 1250 to Grey and 500 to White. Multiplied by 749/3250 these figures become 346 to Gold, 288 to Grey and 115 to White.

Progress totals are now:

Gold	1500 + 366 = 1846
Green	1000 + 214 = 1214
Grey	500 + 285 + 288 = 1073
White	250 + 500 + 115 = 865

None of these candidates has yet reached the quota.

White, having the fewest votes, is eliminated, and his 865 votes are distributed, 760 going to Gold, 65 to Green and 40 to Grey. Gold's total now becomes 1846 + 760 = 2606. Having reached the quota, Gold is the third candidate to be elected.

In Senate elections, votes cast for a particular party are deemed to be for that party's candidates in the order in which they are listed. When six candidates are to be elected for each State, the quota for each candidate is 14.29 per cent of the total formal vote. To elect two candidates requires 28.58 per cent of the vote, and to return three, a party must gain 42.87 per cent. In the 1984 Senate election, as many as 3000 counts were needed in New South Wales to transfer all the preferences and determine the final winner.

WHICH SYSTEM IS BEST?

Most people would agree that a democratic election should meet two important requirements. One is that it should fairly reflect the will of the majority of electors. The other is that it should produce a Government with clear majority support in Parliament. These two aims are not easy to balance.

Simple majority voting is best-suited to a two-party parliamentary system. It is easy to understand, simple to conduct, and gives a quick result. It usually gives the successful party a safe parliamentary majority thus ensuring stable government. Minority parties without a strong regional base and independents without strong local support find it hard to survive.

Preferential voting makes it easier for third or more parties to gain seats or at least influence the outcome of elections, and it gives voters more than one choice. It was introduced in Australia when the Country Party emerged in 1919. The idea was that Nationalist (Liberal) and Country Party candidates would exchange preferences (that is, ask their supporters to give their second preference to the other candidate) so as not to split the anti-Labor vote. Later, it enabled the DLP to keep the Labor Party out of office in Canberra for several years. More recently, Labor has on balance benefited from preferences from the Australian Democrats and the Greens. The advantage is that voters can say to themselves: 'I really want Green, but if I can't have Green, then I prefer White to Black. So my vote for Green will not be wasted if I can help elect White instead.' Preferential voting is a little more complicated than simple majority voting, and counting of votes takes longer, but it also tends to produce a clear majority for one party or coalition of parties.

However, both these systems—being based on single member

electorates—may produce results that do not accurately reflect the overall popular vote. This is because the supporters of the various parties are not evenly distributed throughout a State or the nation. A party whose candidates win by fairly small margins in a large number of electorates will gain more seats than a party which wins more votes in total but whose candidates win by large margins in a smaller number of elector-ates. Similarly, a regional party such as the National Party can win seats while the Australian Democrats, with widely scattered support, may win no seats at all even if they poll more votes overall.

Proportional representation, based on large multi-member electorates, overcomes these inequalities. It enables each party to be represented in Parliament more or less according to the total number of votes it wins. The system is hard to explain, usually produces a large number of invalid votes, and is slow to give results. It is also less personal: people vote for a party list rather than for a local member. Where it has been used in Australia, proportional representation has not led to a proliferation of small parties as in some other countries. Its main drawback here is that it is likely to lead to the two major parties being almost evenly balanced, with minority groups holding the balance of power. It can be argued that such a situation—where a small minority party can frustrate or impose its demands on a majority party—cancels out the advantage claimed for proportional representation: that it reflects the will of the majority of electors.

But to return to the question: which system is best? The answer is that none is perfect, each has advantages and disadvantages, and politicians tend to prefer whichever system suits them best.

MAKING THE VOTER'S TASK EASIER

In every election, many votes are discarded as *informal*. Some voters might deliberately spoil their ballot paper because they do not wish to vote for any of the candidates. If voting were not compulsory they would simply stay at home. Others might object to having to indicate a preference for every candidate or for the particular candidates.

Most informal votes, however, are probably caused by ignorance or carelessness. In Senate elections, where ballot papers might have a list of more than seventy candidates, informal votes sometimes exceeded twelve per cent of the total.

Some voters simply vote 1, 2, 3 and so on down the ballot paper. Candidates whose names appear at the top of a ballot paper have some slight advantage from this so-called *donkey vote*. Parties have even been

A 'How-to-vote' card issued by the Liberal Party for a Federal election, including both Houses.

A 'How-to-vote' card issued by the Australian Labor Party for a State election, for both Houses.

Australian Labor Party.

Please remember to place a number in every square on both Ballot Papers.

How to vote.
You must place a number in every square.

BENDIGO WEST
Legislative Assembly (White Ballot Paper)

1	**KENNEDY, D.**
2	HOLT, R.
3	SANDNER, A.

NORTH WESTERN
Legislative Council (Pink Ballot Paper)

3	EBERY, B.
1	**EDDY, P. J.**
2	WRIGHT, K.

Printed by: Industrial Printing and Publicity Co. Ltd., Richmond.
Authorised by: Peter Batchelor, ALP, 23 Drummond Street, Carlton, 3053

known to choose candidates whose names begin with one of the first letters in the alphabet in the hope of gaining a few extra votes (which in a close contest could make all the difference). To overcome this alphabetical advantage, the order of candidates on ballot papers for the House of Representatives now is decided by a draw in each electorate. In Senate elections, where positions on the ballot paper have long been determined by ballot, the group in first place also benefits from the donkey vote.

The Commonwealth and some States have made voting easier in some ways. Although the Senate ballot paper now looks more complicated, voters are given the choice of simply voting for the party or group they prefer, or of marking preferences for individual candidates as in the past. South Australia has adopted a similar system for its Legislative Council elections. New South Wales has introduced *optional preferential* voting. For the Legislative Assembly, voters need mark only a number 1 for the candidate of their choice, but may indicate further preferences if they wish. For the Legislative Council, preferences need be marked for ten candidates, but not more unless the voter so wishes.

South Australia has made voting for both Houses even simpler. A number 1, tick or cross against a candidate's name on the ballot paper is accepted as a formal vote. For the Legislative Council, voters should mark preferences for as many candidates as are to be elected (usually eleven). If a voter indicates a preference for only one candidate, then the other preferences are allotted according to that candidate's party how-to-vote card if registered with the Electoral Commission.

In Federal and most State elections, candidates now are identified on the ballot paper by their *party affiliation*. Previously, voters had to rely on their memory or on how-to-vote cards given out by party workers. In South Australia, registered how-to-vote cards for each party or group are posted in the polling booths.

How an election is held

Officially, preparations for an election begin with the issue of a writ by the Governor-General or Governor. (Writs for the Senate elections are issued by the Governors in each State. Writs for Legislative Council elections in some States are issued by the President of the Council.) The writ is a command to the returning officers to hold an election, and sets the date for close of nominations of candidates and the polling day. To be eligible for public funds for Federal election campaigns, political parties have to register with the Australian Electoral Commission before the writs are issued.

The political parties, if they have not already done so, select candidates for each electorate they wish to contest, and begin their election campaigns. In the past, each party leader would usually hold a big public meeting at which he announced his policy in a long speech. In recent years, campaigns have tended to open with short but extravagantly produced television programmes in which the leader emphasises only the main points of his party's policy. More detailed policy statements are given to the press. Candidates and their followers hold meetings, send out pamphlets, and often go from house to house in their effort to win support. Party leaders travel to important electorates, 'meet the people', and give media interviews. As the election draws nearer, the parties step up their campaigns with newspaper, radio and television advertisements and publicity. On polling day, party workers give out how-to-vote cards near the polling booths.

Candidates have to lodge a deposit with their nominations to discourage other than serious contestants. In 1993 the deposit was $250 for the House of Representatives and $500 for the Senate. This is refunded to candidates who are elected, and those who win at least four per cent of the total number of formal first preference votes in their electorate. Where a Senate candidate is included in a party or group list, the deposit is refunded if the whole group has won more than four per cent of the first preference votes.

Polling booths are set up at convenient places in each electorate. They are usually open from 8 a.m. to 6 p.m. on the day of the election, normally a Saturday. The officer in charge of each booth has a copy of a roll listing all the people entitled to vote in the electorate.

As electors come in to vote, their name is marked off to ensure that they do not vote more than once. They are given a ballot paper, which they mark in private and drop into a locked box. After the close of voting, the box is unlocked, the votes are counted and the results are sent to a central returning office where totals are compiled by computer. Scrutineers appointed by the candidates or their parties may watch the count but not handle the ballot papers. Ballot papers not properly filled in are classed as informal and are set aside. If necessary, second preferences are counted and distributed. Sometimes it takes a week or longer for final results to be determined. Senate results, which require a great number of counts and calculations, may take several weeks to finish.

Finally, when the result of the election in each electorate is known, the returning officer returns the writ giving the name of the candidate who has been elected.

POSTAL AND ABSENT VOTING

People who are ill or infirm or who are for certain other reasons unable to vote at a polling booth on election day may obtain a postal vote. They

Counting votes at a local polling booth for a Senate election.

must apply to the returning officer before polling day and are issued with a special ballot paper which they fill in and return by post.

People away from their home on polling day may vote as absentees at any other booth. They are given the appropriate ballot paper, which is placed in an envelope and sent back by the returning officer to their electorate.

TIED RESULTS, RECOUNTS AND DISPUTES

If a result is very close, a recount may be ordered. If, after allocation of preferences, two candidates have an equal number of votes, the returning officer has a casting vote. Sometimes, especially if the result is close, a candidate may appeal to a Court of Disputed Returns (a High Court or Supreme Court judge) if he or she can show cause that there have been irregularities to invalidate the election. All this happened in the election for the Nunawading province in Victoria in 1985. The result was tied between the Liberal and Labor candidates. The returning officer decided the result by drawing a name out of a ballot box. The Labor candidate won. But the Liberal candidate decided to challenge the result, not because of the 'lucky dip' draw, but because of alleged polling clerk errors. A Court of Disputed Returns upheld the appeal, declared the election void, and ordered a fresh election for the province. This time the Liberal candidate won.

For further thought

- How often should elections be held? With three yearly elections, it has been said, a Government has one year to settle down, one year to legislate and one year to prepare for the next election. What do you think?
- Should compulsory voting be abolished? Why or why not?
- What are arguments for and against having fewer voters in country electorates than in city electorates?
- Does the electoral system of your State operate to the advantage or disadvantage of any of the major political parties? If so, how?
- Which voting system do you consider to be fairest? Which is most likely to produce a Government with a clear-cut majority? Is it necessary to compromise between the principles of one vote, one value, and the need for stable and workable government?
- Is public funding of political parties the right response to the rising cost of election campaigns? What are the advantages and disadvantages?
- Why should there be, or why should there not be, restrictions on political advertising? Why do you think that public disclosure of donations to political parties is or is not (a) justifiable and (b) likely to be effective?

PARLIAMENT AT WORK

Australia has not only adopted the British system of parliamentary government. It has also inherited the customs, symbols and traditions of the Parliament at Westminster. These are apparent, with only some minor changes, in the ceremonial opening of Parliament, the day-to-day procedures, the titles and dress of the principal parliamentary officers, and even the furnishings of both Houses of Parliament.

This chapter describes Federal Parliament at work. The State Parliaments function in much the same way.

Compared with the original 'provisional' Parliament House, the $1000 million permanent Parliament House opened on Capital Hill, Canberra, on 9 May 1988 is gigantic, with separate entrances for the public, the House of Representatives, the Senate and Ministers and—critics complain—less opportunity to mingle. But as before, separated by a Great Hall, the House of Representatives chamber, furnished in grey-green, is on the left, and the Senate, with a livery of red, is on the right.

PARLIAMENTARY OFFICERS

The seats in each chamber are tiered in a U-shape, the open end facing the elevated chair of the *Speaker* in the House of Representatives and that of the *President* in the Senate. The office of Speaker is ancient and dignified. The Speaker is elected at the beginning of each new Parliament by secret ballot of the members of the House of Representatives. Although usually a member of the governing party, the Speaker is by tradition strictly impartial. The President, elected by ballot by the

Senators every three years, performs a similar role in the Senate. Speakers and Presidents nominated by Labor Governments have usually disregarded the tradition of wearing a full wig and gown.

The Speaker and President control their respective chambers and precincts, preside over meetings of their Houses, and enforce rules of debate and preserve order. Each acts as spokesperson for the particular House and as representative of its powers and dignity.

There is one important difference between the powers of the Speaker and the President. The President may vote, if he or she wishes, on any motion before the Senate, so that the votes of each State remain equal. If the Senate is equally divided, the motion is defeated. The Speaker may vote only if the members in the House are equally divided, and thus has a casting vote.

In each chamber, Government members traditionally sit to the Speaker's or President's right, and Opposition members to the left. Members of other parties sit in the corner benches. Ministers occupy the front benches on the Government side, and leading members of the Opposition—the *shadow Cabinet*—sit on the front benches opposite. Behind the front benches sit the other members, who are often called *backbenchers*.

A large table extends along the centre of each chamber. At the head of each table, below the Speaker or President, sit the *Clerk* and *Clerk-*

The Prime Minister, Mr Paul Keating, speaking in the House of Representatives, with senior Ministers on the front bench behind him.

Assistants. They each wear short grey wigs and black gowns. The Clerk, a permanent official of Parliament, is responsible for keeping a record of proceedings, reading the titles of Bills and documents presented to Parliament, and advising on points of procedure.

Facing each other across the table in the House of Representatives are the Prime Minister and the Leader of the Opposition. Each may be flanked by his deputy. The Prime Minister's place may be taken by the Minister in charge of a Bill or other proceedings before the House, and the Opposition Leader's place by one of the shadow Ministers. In the Senate, the leader of the Government and Opposition leader, and/or their deputies, also sit at the table opposite each other.

Two picturesque figures in Parliament are the *Serjeant-at-Arms* in the House of Representatives and the *Usher of the Black Rod* in the Senate. The Serjeant-at-Arms, wearing a black, long-tailed coat and white bowtie, precedes the Speaker to and from the chamber, carrying the *Mace* on his right shoulder. In the Middle Ages, a mace was a club used instead of a sword by warrior bishops in battle, because bishops were not allowed to shed blood. One of the original tasks of the Serjeant-at-Arms was to

The Serjeant-at-Arms, bearing the Mace.

protect the Speaker. Today the Mace is a symbol of the Speaker's authority, and it is placed on the lower end of the table in the chamber while the Speaker is in the chair. The Mace of the House of Representatives is made of heavily gilded wrought silver, and is surmounted by a crown.

The Usher of the Black Rod, whose dress is similar to that of the Serjeant-at-Arms, attends the President of the Senate. In the House of Lords the office was established by a royal decree by Henry VIII and was traditionally filled by a 'gentleman famous in arms and blood'. The title comes from his staff of office, a black rod, which in Canberra is surmounted with the Australian coat of arms and a silver crown.

The Serjeant-at-Arms and Usher of the Black Rod are both permanent parliamentary officials, and are responsible for maintaining order at the direction of the Speaker or President. They also have some clerical duties.

Another historic office is that of *Whip*. The Whips are members appointed by the parties in each House to ensure that all members are present to vote when need be, to arrange speakers for debates and to act as links between the party leaders and ordinary members. The name 'Whip' comes from a remark by an eighteenth-century statesman, Edmund Burke, who accused his opponents of 'whipping in' their followers to vote in an important debate.

The Usher of the Black Rod.

At the lower side of the table are places for the *Hansard reporters*, who take word-by-word shorthand notes of all proceedings, which are printed after each day's sitting. Thomas Curzon Hansard was a London printer, who in 1803 first printed the parliamentary debates of the House of Commons. The name has lived on, not only in the British Parliament, but also in Parliaments of several Commonwealth countries. Hansard reports form a complete record of parliamentary debates and questions in both Houses of Federal Parliament. Each State Parliament also has its Hansard reports.

Above each of the chambers are galleries for the press and the public. There is also seating for diplomats of other countries, senior Government officials, and special visitors.

The *Parliamentary Press Gallery* refers not merely to the gallery where reporters sit, but also the association of journalists who report parliamentary proceedings and political news in general. In session and out, these journalists, working in offices or from studios in Parliament House, send news from Canberra, directly or indirectly, to every daily newspaper, radio and television station in Australia, and to the world beyond. The most senior and respected political correspondents and commentators wield considerable influence on the course of politics and what the public thinks about the performance of Governments and Oppositions and their leaders.

PARLIAMENTARY BROADCASTS

Proceedings of one or other House in Federal Parliament have been broadcast on radio by the Australian Broadcasting Corporation since 10 July 1946. Parliament took much longer to agree to live television broadcasts. The first occasion on which Parliament was directly televised was the joint sitting of both Houses in August 1974. The Treasurer's Budget speech was telecast for the first time in August 1985. Regular telecasts of question time from the Senate began in August 1990 and from the House of Representatives in February 1991. Radio and television stations may broadcast recorded excerpts from parliamentary debates and statements subject to guidelines laid down by Parliament.

OPENING OF PARLIAMENT

After a general election of the House of Representatives, Parliament must meet within thirty days of the return of the electoral writs. On the morning of the opening day, the Houses meet separately and their Clerks read the proclamation summoning Parliament. The Governor-General does not yet arrive, but sends a Deputy, usually a High Court judge, to prepare for the official opening. The Deputy is admitted to the Senate chamber, where he asks the Usher of the Black Rod, through the Clerk, to request members of the House of Representatives to come to the Senate.

The members file across to the Senate chamber. The Deputy tells both Houses that, before the arrival of the Governor-General, Members and new Senators are to be sworn in, and the Speaker is to be chosen. The Representatives return to their chamber, and presently the Deputy follows them to administer the oath (or affirmation) of allegiance to the Queen. Meanwhile, the President swears in the new Senators. When the Deputy leaves the House, members elect the Speaker. By tradition, the Speaker is dragged to the chair, recalling the days of conflict between the King and the Commons when the position of Speaker was a dangerous one and was accepted reluctantly.

In the afternoon, the Governor-General arrives with due ceremony. After the Speaker has been presented to him or her privately, the Governor-General is ready to open Parliament. The Usher of the Black Rod announces the Governor-General's approach to the Senate. The Governor-General is conducted to the dais, and takes the chair. Black Rod is commanded to let members of the House of Representatives know that the Governor-General 'desires their attendance forthwith'. Black Rod, announced by the Serjeant-at-Arms, delivers this message to the House. The Speaker, preceded by the Serjeant-at-Arms bearing the Mace, leads the Members to the Senate, where they take seats with the Senators.

The Governor-General addresses both Houses. This speech formally announces the reasons for summoning Parliament, but actually outlines the Government's legislative programme for the session. After the Governor-General's speech is given, a copy of it is handed to the President and the Speaker. The Governor-General leaves, and Members of the House of Representatives return to their chamber.

The Houses then each debate the 'address-in-reply', which is a formal expression of loyalty to the Queen and of thanks to the Governor-General for the speech. The House of Representatives follows the traditional practice of the House of Commons of introducing a Bill before the address-in-reply is moved, as a sign of independence. The address-in-reply debate gives Members an opportunity to speak out on any subject and allows new members to make their maiden (first) speeches. When the address-in-reply has been passed in each House, the Speaker and Members and the President and Senators present it personally to the Governor-General at Government House.

The opening of a session begins with both Houses meeting separately to await the arrival of the Governor-General. Members of the House of Representatives are summoned to the Senate chamber, and the procedure is then as for the opening of Parliament.

Queen Elizabeth II is the first monarch to have opened the Federal Parliament in Australia in person. She has done so on three occasions; on 15 February 1954, clad in her richly embroidered Coronation robe; on 28 February 1974; and on 8 March 1977. Although she ceremonially opened the new Parliament House on 9 May 1988, the occasion did not mark the opening of a new Parliament.

A TYPICAL DAY IN PARLIAMENT

How does Parliament go about its daily work? Let us look at an ordinary day in the House of Representatives. The procedure in the Senate and in the State Houses is similar, though not exactly the same. The conduct of business in each House is laid down by a detailed set of rules known as the Standing Orders, which are interpreted and enforced by the Speaker or President.

The ringing of electric bells and flashing of green lights throughout Parliament House summons members to assemble in the House of Representatives. (Senators are summoned by electric buzzers and red flashing lights.) The Speaker takes the chair and reads the *Prayers*, which open each day's sitting.

Question Time is scheduled for 2 p.m. each day, whether the House actually begins sitting just before then or in the morning. 'Are there any Questions Without Notice?' the Speaker asks. Immediately a dozen or so Members spring to their feet to attract the Speaker's attention. This part of the day's proceedings is usually one of the liveliest and most interesting. Members question Ministers on many aspects of government administration, especially on matters of topical interest. The Speaker, so far as possible, alternates the call between Government and Opposition members. Governments and Oppositions often use Question Time to score political points rather than to seek or give genuine information. Sometimes a Minister privately arranges for a Member to ask a certain question to enable the Minister to give a reply that will show up his or her administration in a favourable light; such questions are known among Members as 'Dorothy Dixers'.

Questions that require detailed or long statistical answers may be asked upon notice. They are listed on the daily notice paper and replies are given in writing when the information is available.

After Question Time, which lasts about forty-five minutes, follows the

Presentation of Papers. Ministers 'table' (that is, formally present to Parliament by laying on the table of the House) reports and documents on government activities, such as annual reports of departments or authorities. The Clerk may also have papers to present, such as copies of regulations made under Acts of Parliament. Then follow the *Ministerial Statements*. Ministers, by the unanimous leave of the House, may make statements on matters of public importance. The Minister for Foreign Affairs, for instance, may speak on a crisis in world affairs, or the Minister for Trade may announce an important new trade agreement.

'Are there any *Petitions*?' the Speaker asks next. Any citizen or body of people may use the ancient right to petition Parliament to redress a grievance or to ask it not to go on with some proposal. A petition might, for example, request an increase in pensions, or ask Parliament not to pass a law on divorce. A member who receives a petition has a duty to present it to the House, if it is respectfully worded in the form set out in the Standing Orders. The Clerk reads it out.

Any member may propose to the Speaker by noon on a sitting day that a definite *Matter of Public Importance* be submitted to the House for discussion. This enables the Opposition and sometimes Government backbenchers to raise topics of their own choosing for debate. The proposal must be supported by eight members (five members in the

Senate), and time for discussion is limited to two hours (three hours in the Senate). This procedure is used nearly every sitting day by the Opposition to criticise particular aspects of Government policy or administration.

Another opportunity for private members to raise matters of interest to them—whether of national importance or of concern to someone in their electorate—is *Grievance Day*. The technical question put forward for debate is 'that grievances be noted' and it is allowed for on the notice paper on every second Thursday that Parliament is sitting. Each member may speak for ten minutes.

The House is now ready to begin or resume the Business of the Day as listed on the notice paper. Each item is listed as a *motion on notice* (a motion of which notice has been given on the previous day of sitting) or an order of the day, such as the continuation of a debate. Each day's business is arranged by the *Leader of the House* (a senior Minister) after consulting the Opposition.

At about 11.30 p.m., the debate before the House, if it has not ended, may be adjourned. A Minister then moves the *Adjournment of the House*. On this motion, any matter at all may be debated, and members can raise any matter on which they feel the Government should act. Finally, the Speaker adjourns the House to the next day of sitting.

HOW AN ACT OF PARLIAMENT IS MADE

Laws made by Parliament begin as Bills. A Bill is a proposal for a law, which, when it passes both Houses and receives Royal Assent, becomes an Act of Parliament, or statute.

As we have seen, almost all Bills are *Government Bills*. They stem from Government policy or from recommendations made by government departments or even from suggestions made by Members of Parliament. In each case, Cabinet authorises a Minister to have a Bill prepared. The Bill is drawn up in the necessary legal form by the Parliamentary Draftsman.

Any member of Parliament may sponsor and introduce a Bill, but such *Private Member's Bills* are few. They are rarely passed.

Bills may originate in either House, but most begin in the lower House. Money Bills (to authorise the spending of government funds or to impose taxes or charges) must originate in the lower House and on the motion of a Minister.

Every Bill, to succeed, must go through six stages in each House. These are:

1 initiation;
2 first reading;
3 second reading;
4 consideration in committee;
5 adoption of the report from the committee;
6 third reading.

Each reading, if the House votes in favour of it, means that the Clerk simply reads out the title of the Bill. The Bill has then passed that stage. The initiation and the three readings should take place on separate days, but often the House agrees to suspend the Standing Orders to enable a Bill to pass more quickly.

A Bill is initiated when a Member, usually a Minister, gives notice that, at the next day of sitting, that Member will move that he or she have leave to bring in a Bill for an Act to —— (then follows the title of the Bill). At the next sitting, the Member moves the motion, which is usually agreed to. The first reading follows immediately, without debate, enabling the Bill to be circulated and the contents to be made known.

At the second reading, the general principles of the Bill are explained and debated. If the Bill is a Government Bill, the Opposition usually obtains an adjournment of the debate to allow its Members to study it. The debate ends with a vote on the question 'that this Bill be now read a second time'.

If the vote is in the affirmative, the Bill is then dealt with in Committee of the Whole House. The Speaker leaves the chamber and the Mace is placed under the table until the Speaker returns. The *Chairman of Committees*, a senior Member elected to this post at the beginning of each Parliament, takes the chair at the head of the table next to the Clerk. This procedure recalls the reign of the Stuarts, when the Speaker was often too closely associated with the King, and the Commons preferred to discuss the details of a Bill in the Speaker's absence, that is, *in committee*. During the committee stage, a Bill is considered clause by clause, and detailed amendments may be made.

When this has been done, the Speaker returns and the Mace is replaced on the table. The Chairman of Committees reports the work of the committee to the Speaker, who asks the House to adopt the report.

On the motion that the Bill be read a third time, the Bill may be, but usually is not, debated again as a whole. If the House agrees to the third reading, the Bill has passed all stages.

The Bill is now sent to the other House, where it goes through the same procedure. If the other House amends the Bill, it must go back to the House from which it came, where the amendments must be approved.

When the Bill has finally passed both Houses, it is presented to the Governor-General (in the States, to the Governor) for Royal Assent.

The Governor-General may propose amendments, but normally does not do so, except on the advice of his Ministers and even then only to correct a mistake or to clarify some provision. When assent has been given, the Bill is an Act of Parliament. Usually it comes into force immediately, but sometimes it does not become law until a date named in the Act or proclaimed by the Government.

DELEGATED LEGISLATION

Often, to save time, Parliament delegates to the Government a limited power of legislation—the power to make regulations. Parliament passes an Act setting out the general principles of desired law, leaving the administrative details to regulation. Regulations are formally made by the Governor-General (or Governor) in Council and are known as delegated or subordinate legislation. They must be notified in the Government Gazette.

As government activity is ever-increasing in scope and complexity, the amount of delegated legislation has grown tremendously. Many people feel that this is weakening the authority of Parliament and giving too

much power to the executive arm. A safeguard against this tendency is that all Federal regulations must be laid before each House of Parliament. Either House can vote to disallow any regulation. All regulations are also examined by the Senate Regulations and Ordinances Committee, to ensure that they are in accordance with the Act under which they are made and that they do not unduly trespass on personal rights and liberties. Some States, particularly Victoria, do not provide so carefully for parliamentary control of delegated legislation.

THE BUDGET AND MONEY BILLS

The Budget is the Government's yearly financial statement of income and expenditure. The Treasurer usually presents it to Parliament in August or September. In the Budget speech, the Treasurer outlines the proposed income from taxes, loans and other sources, and estimated expenditure to meet the cost of government activities for the financial year. Detailed estimates, prepared by the Treasury on information given by the departments, are presented to Members to show how the money is to be spent.

The Government is not allowed to spend money or to impose taxes without the consent of Parliament. Parliament grants the money needed by the Government by passing *Appropriation Bills.* Most government income, other than loan money, is paid into the Consolidated Revenue Fund, and it is from this fund that an annual appropriation is made to meet the ordinary cost of public services and administration. A separate Appropriation Bill is needed to authorise the spending on loan money (money borrowed by the Government), which is used mainly for public works and development projects.

As the Appropriation Bills are not passed until after the Budget is presented some months after the beginning of each financial year, Parliament before the end of June passes *Supply Bills* to provide money needed during the interval. Parliament must also pass separate *Bills to Impose Taxation.* All these Bills must originate in the lower House.

In theory, it is still the Sovereign, represented here by the Governor-General, who asks Parliament for grants of money. The Budget is introduced in the House of Representatives in the form of a message from the Governor-General to the Speaker, setting out detailed Estimates of Expenditure, and recommending that the necessary appropriation be made. After the Speaker has read out the message to the House, the Treasurer, as the responsible Minister, introduces an Appropriation Bill, which is then debated and dealt with like any other Bill. Supply Bills are similarly dealt with, except that they are based not on Estimates but on simple recommendations from the Governor-General.

Once passed by the House of Representatives, all money Bills must be sent to the Senate for approval. The Senate may pass or reject, but not amend, such Bills. However, it may suggest amendments to the House of Representatives. If the Senate were to reject an important money Bill, the Government would be bound to resign and a double dissolution would probably follow. In 1975, the Senate deferred passage of the Appropriation Bills arising from the Budget in an attempt to bring down the Labor Government, which did not have a majority in the Senate. The Governor-General intervened in the crisis, dismissed the Government, decided on a double dissolution, and appointed the Opposition Leader as head of a caretaker administration until the elections were held.

CONDUCT OF DEBATES

Members of the House of Representatives (and the lower Houses of the States) are referred to in the House, not by their names, but by titles, such as 'the Honourable Member for Capricornia' (the electorate he or she represents) or the 'Right Honourable Prime Minister'.

Sometimes a Member may be heard to refer to 'another place'. This is the traditional way of referring to the other House, which is never mentioned by name, recalling the historic hostility between the House of Commons and the House of Lords.

DIVISIONS

Vote on a motion, such as one that a Bill be read a second time, are decided by a majority of voices, 'Aye' or 'No'. The presiding officer announces the result, but if his or her opinion is challenged, a division is held. The Clerk rings the division bells and turns a two-minute sand glass. The bells summon Members who are outside the chamber, and enable any who wish to abstain from voting to leave. When the two minutes are up, the doors are closed. Members take seats on the side of the House on which they intend to vote, the 'Ayes' moving to the right of the Chair, and the 'Noes' to the left. Tellers (Members appointed by the Chair) mark on printed lists how each Member voted, and tally up the result.

TIME LIMITS

The Standing Orders limit the time a Member may speak in debates. Time limits are more generous in the Senate, the House of review, where there are fewer Members. There are two other ways of limiting the time of debates—the '*guillotine*' and the '*closure*' or '*gag*'. The guillotine is a resolution that a certain time be allotted to each or any stage of a Bill or other business. The gag simply ends a debate on a resolution, which may be moved by any Member at any time that the question be now put. The matter before the House is decided at once. These tactics are often used by the Government, which has the numbers to carry them out, to speed up the passage of legislation. In the House of Representatives a Member may be 'gagged' on a resolution that he be 'no longer heard'.

PARLIAMENTARY PRIVILEGE

Parliamentary privilege means the special rights of Parliament and its members which ensure the independence of Parliament and enables its work to be carried out without hindrance or fear of prosecution. The most important parliamentary privilege is freedom of speech. The famous Bill of Rights of 1688, which set out the conditions on which the British throne was offered to William and Mary, declared: 'That the freedom of speech, and debates or proceedings in Parliament, ought not to be impeached or questioned in any court or place out of Parliament.'

No matter what Members say in Parliament, they cannot be sued for slander or libel for their statements, which are absolutely privileged. They are subject only to the rules of the House. Papers and documents published by the authority of either House, including Hansard reports, are similarly protected. Newspaper reports of parliamentary proceedings have qualified privilege: they are protected only if they are fair and accurate.

It is a breach of privilege to coerce or impede a Member of Parliament or to bring Parliament into contempt. In a notable case in June 1955 the House of Representatives committed two men, the proprietor of a Sydney suburban newspaper and a journalist, to gaol for three months, after finding them guilty of a serious breach of privilege by having published defamatory articles about a Member of Parliament.

THE OMBUDSMAN

From Sweden has come the concept of the Ombudsman, or Parliamentary Commissioner, as a 'watchdog' of citizens' rights. Appointed by Parliament and independent of the Government, the Ombudsman investigates complaints by private citizens and organisations against oppressive, wrongful or unjust decisions or actions by government authorities or officials. The Ombudsman may try to remedy injustices or mistakes by direct intervention, or report directly to Parliament.

Western Australia was the first Australian State to appoint an Ombudsman, in 1972, followed by the other States and the Northern Territory. The Federal Government appointed an Ombudsman in 1977. The Ombudsman can investigate complaints about any areas of Commonwealth administration as well as initiate inquiries. There is also an Ombudsman for the defence forces.

For further thought

- Do Governments give Parliament enough time to discuss important legislation and affairs of state?
- Do the traditions inherited from Westminster add to the dignity of Australian Parliaments? Is the behaviour of members of Parliament in keeping with those traditions?
- How valuable is Question Time as a means of keeping Governments accountable and on their toes? To what extent has this period been misused for political purposes by Governments and Oppositions?
- Do you think broadcasting of parliamentary proceedings is worthwhile or a waste of time? Should televising of proceedings be confined to important occasions?
- Some Members of Parliament feel an Ombudsman is unnecessary, because they—or in more serious cases, the courts—are available to deal with individual grievances. What do you think? Should there be separate Ombudsmen to deal with complaints against police and local government authorities?

8

GOVERNMENT AT WORK

The Government of Australia and its States and Territories is headed by small groups of Ministers, who are responsible to their Parliaments and so to the people. For the day-to-day work of administration and provision of government services they rely on public servants. These are the officers and employees of various government departments. Many others, who are not public servants in the strict sense, also carry out the daily tasks of government. They include railway employees, teachers and police.

An indication of the growth of government is the great increase in the number of people employed in Australia by government authorities of all kinds. If those employed by local government authorities are included, then about three persons in every ten of the working population were public sector employees in 1990. In 1900 the proportion was one in twenty. Most Governments are now trying to reduce the number of people they employ.

The Public Service is sometimes called the *bureaucracy*, because it is hierarchical in structure and works according to established rules and procedures. Strictly speaking, the term should not be confined to government service. Many big businesses are also organised in a bureaucratic way.

ORGANISATION

GOVERNMENT DEPARTMENTS

In recent years there have been significant changes in the organisation of the Australian (formerly Commonwealth) Public Service, other government authorities and their relationship with the Government of the day. Similar changes are also occurring in the States to a greater or lesser extent.

First, let's look at the traditional model as inherited from Britain and then let's examine some of the changes. The concept was that Governments would each be served by an independent, impartial, anonymous, career Public Service, whose members were recruited as school leavers or graduates by competitive examination, and promoted on merit (or mixture of merit and seniority). They were employed by a Public Service Board and paid according to their classification and grade. They could move from department to department, and expect to spend a lifetime in the service (with little fear of dismissal or retrenchment) and retire on a generous pension.

Governments and Ministers would come and go, but the Public Service would continue to serve without fear or favour, providing continuity, experience and expertise regardless of the political affiliation of its masters. Each Minister was in charge of a department, or perhaps more than one department. It was his or her duty to ensure that the department carried out the policy of the Government and administered the laws passed by Parliament. Then, as they are now, Ministers were the parliamentary heads of their departments, but each department also had a permanent head usually known as the Secretary or Director.

The relationship of the Minister to the permanent head was never simply that of the chief to a second-in-command. Ministers could decide and direct, but their permanent heads would be expected to advise as well as carry out instructions. Some senior public servants, such as the heads of the Prime Minister's Department, Treasury and Foreign Affairs, still have a great influence on government policy. After all, they are the professionals; Ministers are usually amateurs and non-specialist in the field of activities for which they are responsible. The Public Service often initiates proposals for legislation or action, but Ministers, individually or collectively, have to judge whether such suggestions are publicly acceptable, politically prudent or financially affordable.

So what has altered, for better or for worse?

• There are now more Ministers than departments. The Keating Government elected in 1993 appointed thirty Ministers to take charge of eighteen departments. Nearly thirty former separate departments had already been amalgamated into a smaller number of 'mega-departments', with shared ministerial responsibility (such as Foreign Affairs *and* Trade), or a senior Minister and two or more junior Ministers assisting or taking responsibility for particular sections of the department.

• Departmental heads are no longer 'permanent'. Incoming Governments and even new Ministers after a Cabinet reshuffle now tend to appoint chief executives from within the Public Service or from outside whom they believe to be sympathetic to the Government's political goals and priorities, and with whom they feel they work well personally. As a result, the Public Service at the top has become more 'politicised' as in the United States and less independent and impartial as in the British tradition.

• Governments and Ministers no longer rely solely on the advice of their departments and its heads on policy and how to carry it out. There has been a growth in the appointment of ministerial advisers and personal staff who are not public servants. They are chosen for their professional expertise or political loyalty (usually both), and may hold their position only as long as the Government or their Minister does.

• The Public Service is no longer exclusive in its higher ranks. Not only departmental heads but also the senior executive service—numbering about 1500 senior executive and professional officers—may be appointed directly from outside the service to tap into a broader range of management and specialist skills available from private enterprise, the professions and academic life. This development has also increased the politicisation of the service, as officials in tune with Government policy may be favoured to be chosen or promoted. In Victoria, the Kennett Government has decided to employ senior officials on short-term contracts.

• Australian public servants below the rank of departmental head (who have always been appointed by the Government) are now employed by their individual departments instead of the Public Service Board, which was abolished in 1987. Subject to Government policy and guidelines laid down by a new Public Service Commissioner with limited powers, departmental heads may create and abolish positions, and are now more fully responsible for the management, resources and efficiency of their departments.

• Departmental heads and statutory officers like the Taxation Commissioner are not as anonymous as they once were. Some have become well-known public figures and some have become involved in political controversy. Sometimes a former political adviser is appointed as a departmental head or to the senior executive service.

The following list is a rough guide to the main functions of the Federal and Victorian Government departments. As you will see, some do not fit neatly under a single heading. The Victorian departments are fairly typical of those of other States, although there are differences in each State.

FEDERAL	VICTORIA

1 Policy and coordination

Prime Ministers and Cabinet	Premier and Cabinet
Treasury	Treasury
Foreign Affairs and Trade	Transport
Defence	Planning and Development
Health, Housing, Local Government and Community Services	

2 Development and conservation

Employment, Education and Training	Business and Employment
Industry Technology and Regional Development	Planning and Development
	Energy and Minerals
Primary Industries	Agriculture
Immigration and Ethnic Affairs	Conservation and Natural Resources
Environment, Sport and Territories	Arts, Sport and Tourism
Tourism	

3 Regulation and revenue

Treasury (Taxation)	Treasury
Finance	Finance
Industrial Relations	Transport (VicRoads)

4 Security and order

Attorney-General	Justice
Defence	Police and Emergency Services

5 Direct services and welfare

Health, Housing, Local Government and Community Services	Health and Community Services
	Planning and Development (Housing)
Social Security	Education
Education and Training	
Veterans' Affairs	

6 Communications

Transport and Communications	Transport

7 Territories and administration

Arts and Administrative Services	Planning and Development
Environment, Sport and Territories	Arts, Sport and Tourism

STATUTORY BODIES

Not all the work of government is done by departments. Much of it is carried out by a variety of statutory bodies. As the word *statutory* implies, they are set up for particular purposes by statutes (legislation) which give them separate legal status and define their structure and function. They are directed by boards or commissions appointed for fixed terms by the Government.

As you will understand when you examine what such bodies do, the idea is to give them independence from day-to-day ministerial control. Some are really government businesses, and need to be run as such by people with specialist skills, and free from the normal public service constraints. Others need to be impartial and free from political interference. In practice, they all differ a great deal in their degree of autonomy, their relationship with the Government of the day, and their powers and revenue resources.

The biggest and most important are the statutory corporations, both Federal and State, established to run *government business enterprises and developmental undertakings*. These include postal services, railways, Government airlines and ships, trams and buses, Government banks, electricity and gas supplies, water supplies and irrigation, main roads and harbours.

Examples of statutory bodies in this category are:

Federal: Australian Broadcasting Corporation, Australian National Line, Australian National Railways Commission, Australian Postal Commission (Australia Post), Qantas Airways, Snowy Mountains Hydro-electric Authority.

Victoria: Gas and Fuel Corporation, Melbourne Water, Port of Melbourne Authority, Public Transport Commission, Roads Corporation, State Electricity Commission.

The Federal and some State Governments are engaged in selling the whole or parts of their government business enterprises to private enterprise, either directly or by turning them into public companies and selling a proportion of the shares to the public. This process is called privatisation. For example, the Commonwealth Bank of Australia, which absorbed the State Bank of Victoria, is now a public company in which the Federal Government still owns a majority of shares. Similarly, the NSW Government sold its Government Insurance Office, which now operates as a commercial insurance company, GIO, and has in turn bought Victoria's former State Insurance Office. Telecom Australia is no longer a government monopoly and is likely to be privatised. Qantas Airways has been merged with Australian Airlines in readiness for being wholly or partly sold.

A second group of statutory authorities is concerned with the *marketing of primary products*, within Australia and for export. The Federal Government has set up the Australian Wheat **Board** and the Australian Wool, Dairy, Dried Fruits, Meat and Livestock, Pork, and Wine and Brandy **Corporations**. The States also have **marketing boards** for milk, eggs, dairy products, potatoes, onions, barley, maize, dried fruits, rice and other products.

The many other statutory bodies, mainly in the States, are more difficult to classify according to function or form. They include:

- **Regulatory and coordinating authorities,** such as the Reserve Bank, Insurance and Superannuation Commission, Prices Surveillance Commission, Australian Telecommunications Authority (AUSTEL), Environment Protection Authorities and Public Service Commissioners;
- **Semi-judicial bodies,** such as Trade Practices Commission, Administrative Appeals Commission and Equal Opportunity Boards;
- **Boards for regulation of professional and occupational standards** (registration or examination of doctors, dentists, teachers, nurses, chemists, surveyors, plumbers and others);
- **Research authorities and institutions,** such as the Australian Bureau of Statistics, the Commonwealth Scientific and Industrial Research Organisation (CSIRO) and the Institute of Criminology;
- **Educational, cultural, recreational trusts,** for public libraries, art galleries, museums, parks and gardens, sport, zoos and cemeteries.

There are also a large number of **non-statutory advisory committees,** not established by legislation but appointed by Ministers or departments to provide specialist and expert advice, or to represent community interests (such as on matters of public health, education, welfare, business and economic affairs, or cultural matters and ethnic affairs).

All these bodies vary greatly in the form of their governing authority, the nature and scope of their powers, control of finances and method of staffing. They differ from the departments mainly in having greater freedom from ministerial control over their administration, although they are subject to Government control on matters of major policy. Most of the bigger statutory corporations have their own income from earnings or special taxes and keep separate accounts on business lines; have control of their own staffs, who are not subject to public service regulations; and are better able than a department to plan ahead without interference. Various interests can be represented on the boards; producers, for example, are represented on the marketing boards.

The term *quango*—coined in England and short for quasi-autonomous national government organisation—is sometimes applied to the bewildering number and variety of statutory and non-statutory bodies that have been created over the years. A Senate committee in 1993 identified 358 Commonwealth statutory authorities and 397 non-statutory offices and advisory committees. In an earlier report, the committee reported that many such bodies had outlived their usefulness or could be more appropriately incorporated in a department. It also suggested that when a Government establishes new bodies, it should add a 'sunset clause' in the enabling legislation. This is a clause to provide that an authority automatically ceases to exist after a certain period unless Parliament makes a positive decision at the time to continue it. The Victorian Parliament some years ago established a Public Bodies Review Committee to investigate some 7000 state qangos, with the aim of either eliminating them or making them more accountable and efficient.

The problem of the independence of statutory corporations from political pressure is a thorny one. Take the railways, for instance. There is a conflict in outlook, as one critic has observed, between those who want to see the railways run as a social service and those who want to see it run as a business enterprise. On one hand, the railways are under constant pressure to keep fares and freights low and to run trains where and when they are little used. On the other hand, the transport authorities may be keen to operate the railways efficiently and economically, so that, as far as possible, they 'pay their way'. In practice, the corporations try to strike a balance between the demands of sectional interests and the desire for economy and efficiency.

One way of reconciling the conflict is for the statutory corporations to be run on commercial principles with 'user-pays' pricing policies, and to be reimbursed by the Government for 'community service obligations'; that is, for providing affordable services in remote areas or providing discounts for pensioners or students.

ADVISORY COMMISSIONS AND COMMITTEES OF INQUIRY

These bodies, which exist to give Governments independent and impartial advice in particular fields, are broadly of three kinds. Some are long-established and continue regardless of changes of Government. For example, the Grants Commission was set up in 1933 to recommend special grants to needy States and now advises on how Federal grants should be shared among the States so as to ensure that all can afford a national standard of services. The Industries Commission, which has changed in name over the years, advises on government assistance (such as through tariffs and bounties) to Australian industries. The Australia Council advises on Federal grants to literature and the arts.

The second class of more short-lived advisory bodies may be established by a particular Government to advise on new policies and allocation of funds, but are likely to be abolished by a succeeding Government. The Whitlam Government (1972–75) made extensive use of special commissions and committees of inquiry, which were mostly disbanded by the Fraser Government (1975–83) that followed it.

Federal and State Governments have long made use of commissions or committees of inquiry to investigate and report on particular subjects. They may be headed by a judge or expert in a particular field, and may hold public hearings of evidence from interested people and organisations. Federal inquiries set up or held in recent years include those into poverty, population, taxation, national superannuation, Australian Government administration, intelligence and security, human relationships, drug trafficking and Aboriginal deaths in custody.

THE COST OF GOVERNMENT

The tremendous amount and variety of work done by the Federal and State Governments requires enormous amounts of money, totalling some thousands of millions of dollars a year. As everyone in the community benefits from the work of government, all who are able must contribute towards its cost.

Most of the money needed comes from taxes of various kinds. Some of it comes from the earnings of government business enterprises. A small part derives from other sources, such as interest, fines and fees, and the sale and lease of lands. All this government income is called *revenue*, and is paid by each Government into a *Consolidated Revenue Fund*.

Not all government income is from revenue. Governments also borrow money, both within Australia and overseas. The *loan money* goes into *Loan Funds* and is usually used to pay for capital works, such as the building of new schools, hospitals and dams. Interest has to be paid on the loans from revenue each year, and some revenue may be put aside in a sinking fund to repay the loans. The justification for the use of borrowed money is twofold. First, if the loans are used for community assets that will benefit future generations, it is considered fair for the cost to be spread over a long period rather than to be borne by taxpayers all at once. Second, if the loans are used for works that will earn revenue or lead to increased production, such as power stations, roads and reservoirs for irrigation, then the investment is well worthwhile.

However, Governments in recent years have tended to spend much more than they collect in taxes, and have had to use Loan Funds to make up their deficits, that is, to use borrowed money to pay for day-to-day expenses such as wages and salaries. This cannot go on indefinitely, and the Victorian Government, to name one, is now trying to reduce its growing debt by cutting back on expenditure and reducing the number of public employees.

Each Government also has a *Trust Fund* in which accounts are held for special purposes outside ordinary departmental expenses, and other moneys held for future use.

Since 1942, the Federal Government has collected all personal income tax in Australia and made financial assistance grants, formerly called tax reimbursements, to the States each year. The basis of these grants has changed from time to time. From 1976 to 1985 it was an agreed proportion of annual personal income tax collections. From 1985, new arrangements were introduced to give the States greater financial stability and allow for higher prices and some growth in responsibilities. The exact amounts are formally determined by the Premiers' Conference every year, usually in June or July, but largely decided by the Commonwealth. The Northern Territory now receives grants on a similar basis, and the Federal Government also provides financial assistance grants for local government.

In addition to 'untied' financial assistance grants, which the States may spend as they wish, the Federal Government also makes 'tied' or specific purpose grants under Section 96 of the Constitution. This is money, whether for capital works or running costs, which must be used by the States for purposes such as schools, colleges, housing, roads, urban transport and regional development, and perhaps on detailed conditions that the Commonwealth prescribes.

The Federal Government may also make special grants to States that are financially weaker or have particular short-term problems, such as flood, bushfire or drought relief. Such grants may be recommended by the Grants Commission, which also advises on how financial assistance grants should be allocated among the States.

Soon after the beginning of every financial year, each Government draws up a *Budget*, setting out how much money it expects to receive and spend during the year. Budgets have tended to get bigger over the years, as Governments have to provide more works and services for the growing population and as the general level of prices and wages has risen. Governments have also expanded their range of activities, particularly in economic affairs, social security and development. Federal expenditure has risen from $198 million in 1938–39 to $100 000 million in 1992–93.

The Federal Government, in framing its Budget, now considers not only its own needs but also those of the economy as a whole. It may, for instance, budget for a deficit (plan to spend more than it expects to receive), especially in times of economic recession. It may do this, for example, to provide for more employment by spending more on public works and job training; to help industry by reducing taxation, thus lowering costs to encourage investment; or to expand social security and education. In good times, the Government may budget for a surplus to reduce debt and the need for borrowings.

The Federal Government now generally presents an economic statement or 'mini-Budget' some months before the normal Budget to give advance notice of proposed tax changes, new spending initiatives or cuts in expenditure.

TAXATION

Taxation is of two types, direct and indirect.

Direct taxes are levied directly on the income or assets of individuals and companies. The main Federal direct tax is income tax, while State direct taxes include payroll tax and land tax. Personal income tax is graded according to ability to pay. People with low incomes pay nothing, or very little, while those with higher incomes pay progressively more.

Income tax, which provides for more than half of the Federal tax revenue, is paid both by individuals and companies. Payroll tax, originally introduced as a Federal tax to pay for child endowment (now called family allowances), is paid by employers whose annual wage bills exceed a certain sum. Land tax is based on the unimproved value of land.

There are two other, more controversial forms of direct tax. The States and Commonwealth have phased out one of these, namely probate or estate duties, which were formerly levied on the value of properties and possessions whose owners had died, and gift duties, which were intended to prevent people from avoiding death duties by giving their property to relatives during their lifetime. Although these taxes have become very unpopular, they are regarded by some people as among the fairest of all taxes. However, in 1985, the Federal Government introduced the second type, a capital gains tax, for the first time in Australia. This is a tax levied on the increase in value of property, investments and certain valuable possessions from the time of acquisition to the date of sale or disposal, less an allowance for inflation.

Taxes based on ability to pay are regarded as fairer than those which are not. Governments often prefer to rely heavily on income tax because it can be deducted from wages and salaries (called PAYE, or pay-as-you-earn deductions), and because the amount collected tends to rise faster than the rate of inflation as more and more taxpayers are pushed into higher tax brackets.

Indirect taxes are included in the prices of many goods and services we buy. The Government collects these taxes from the people who make and sell the goods and provide the service. The tax on each item is simpl added to the price paid by the customer, who thus pays indirectly, often without knowing it. The main indirect taxes levied by the Federal Government are customs and excise duties and sales tax. These are sometimes called consumption taxes because they are levied on what people spend or use rather than on what they earn or own.

Customs duties (or tariffs) are paid on many goods imported from overseas. Revenue from this source is diminishing as the Federal Government is committed to reducing tariff protection for Australian industries to make them competitive by world standards. Excise is levied on certain goods produced in Australia, mainly beer and spirits, tobacco and cigarettes. Petrol refined in Australia pays excise, while imported petrol pays customs duty. Sales tax is imposed at the wholesale level at different rates on hundreds of goods from cameras to motor cars, which are regarded as less essential than basic foodstuffs and household necessities. The Federal coalition parties were in favour of introducing a more broadly based goods and services tax (GST) to replace sales tax and a number of other taxes. After its unexpected defeat in the 1993 election, the coalition dropped its commitment to the GST.

In contrast to direct taxes, indirect taxes are regressive: they fall more heavily on the poor than on the rich. A tax on cigarettes takes a bigger slice of a poor person's income than a rich person's, and as there are more people on low incomes, most of the revenue comes from this group. One can, of course, avoid the tax by not smoking, but this knowledge is little comfort for the confirmed smoker.

Forms of indirect taxation imposed by the States include motor registration and driver's licence fees, stamp duties on property transfers and other documents, bank transactions, liquor licence fees, and taxes on ing and lotteries.

Taxation is also used by Governments for purposes other than to raise nue. Governments can influence the economy by raising or lowering level of taxation (and by increasing or curtailing government ling). Progressive income tax helps to even out extremes of wealth. ct taxes may be used to control spending on luxury goods and to rage excessive drinking, smoking and gambling. Many customs ave been imposed to protect Australian manufacturers (and thus ment of Australian workers) from competition of cheaper l goods.

AL CONTROL

ernment relies on the *Treasury* to prepare and carry out its programme as expressed in the Budget. Towards the end of each year, the Treasury calls for estimates of revenue and expenditure

FEDERAL BUDGET 1985–86

Estimated outlays	$m.	Estimated receipts	$m.
1 Defence	9 885.5	**Taxation Revenue**	
2 Education	9 200.5	Income Tax	
3 Health	14 761.6	Individuals	
4 Social Security and Welfare	37 943.2	Gross PAYE	43 945
5 Housing and Community Amenities	1 426.5	Refunds	4 785
6 Culture and Recreation	1 270.7		
7 Economic Services		Net PAYE	39 160
A. Transport and Communication	2 694.0	Other	6 445
B. Industry Assistance and Development	3 310.7	Medicare Levy	2 505
C. Labour and Employment	2 726.7	Prescribed Payment system	1 300
D. Other Economic Services	301.9		
		Total Individuals	49 410
Total Economic Services	**9 033.3**		
		Companies	12 110
8 General Public Services		Superannuation Funds	1 200
A. Legislative Services	438.8	Withholding Tax	870
B. Law, Order and Public Safety	928.3	Petroleum Resource Rent Tax	1 200
C. Foreign Affairs and Overseas Aid	1 950.9	Fringe Benefits Tax	1 380
D. General and Scientific Research	988.7		
E. Administrative Services	3 188.7	**Total Income Tax**	66 170
		Sales Tax	9 440
Total General Public Services	7 495.5	Excise Duty -	
		Petroleum Products	7 260
9 Not Allocated to Function		Other	2 350
A. Assistance to Other Govts nec	14 070.9	Customs Duty -	
B. Public Debt Interest	6 406.4	Imports	3 540
C. Contingency Reserve	–	Coal Exports	–
D. Asset Sales	–1 600.0	Debits Tax	–
		Other Taxes, Fees and Fines	1 683
Total Not Allocated to Function	18 877.3		
		Total Taxation Revenue	90 443
TOTAL OUTLAYS	109 894.0		
		Non-Tax Revenue	
		Interest	2 490
		Dividends and Other	3 572
		Total Non-Tax Revenue	6 062
		TOTAL REVENUE	96 505

from all departments for the coming year. Estimates of expenditure are carefully examined and, if necessary, revised to bring them into line with expected income and Government policy. Cabinet, of course, has the final say before the Budget is presented to Parliament.

Once the Budget has been approved by Parliament, the Finance Department has to see that the departments conform to it. It does this by controlling the Consolidated Revenue Fund, Loan Fund and other special funds, and by keeping accounts of all Government income and spending. After the end of the financial year, the Treasury prepares a statement of receipts and expenditure to be presented to Parliament.

An independent check on the honesty and efficiency of the Treasury, Finance Department and Government is provided by the *Auditor-General*, who may be described as Parliament's 'watchdog'. Although the Auditor-General, in the Commonwealth and in each State, is appointed by the Government, the position is directly responsible to Parliament. The Auditor-General audits all Government accounts, as well as those of the statutory corporations not under Finance Department control, and this report accompanies the Treasurer's annual statement of receipts and expenditure to Parliament. Where necessary, the Auditor-General reports on examples of waste, extravagance or inefficiency.

The Federal and most State Parliaments have a further financial control in the *Public Accounts Committees*, which investigate activities of particular departments and authorities, and examine accounts and reports of the Auditor-General. *Public Works Committees* examine proposals for capital expenditure on new works projects before they are approved by the Government.

THE NATIONAL DEBT

This is the sum of all borrowed money owed by the Federal and State including Northern Territory) Governments. Money borrowed on overnment securities totalled $60 883 million in June 1992 (about 00 per head of population), compared with $2690 million in 1939 ut $400 per head of population). Interest charges in 1991–92 were 9 million. The table on the following page shows the increase in the al debt since the beginning of the Second World War.

u consider the increase in population and the decline in the value through inflation, the growth in the national debt is not as huge ht seem. The big increase in the Commonwealth debt between 1949 was for money raised for the war effort. In the 1950s and ost Commonwealth capital works were financed from revenue, lmost all of the loan money raised in Australia and overseas for s' public works. In recent years, however, the biggest increase has

Year	Commonwealth Debt ($ million)	States' Debt ($ million)	Total ($ million)
1939	686	2 004	2 690
1949	3 684	2 202	5 886
1959	3 512	4 988	8 500
1969	3 682	8 301	12 513
1979	17 405	13 681	31 086
1989	41 387	17 840	59 232
1992	47 327	13 555	60 883

been in Commonwealth borrowings, some of which has been given to the States in the form of interest-free, non-repayable grants. In recent years, the national debt as a proportion of gross domestic product (GDP)—that is, the size of the domestic economy, or total value of goods and services produced in Australia—has fallen from 26.3 per cent in 1986 to 15.3 per cent in 1992.

The *Australian Loan Council* was set up in 1927 to coordinate the borrowings of the Federal and State Governments. Since 1936, it has also approved the borrowings for statutory ('semi-government') and local government authorities. The council consists of the Prime Minister and the six State Premiers and Chief Minister of the Northern Territory (or Ministers representing them). As the States have one vote in any decision, and the Commonwealth two, plus a casting vote, the Federal Government has been able to dominate Loan Council decisions, provided it could win the support of two States.

In the early 1980s, the importance of the Loan Council declined as some types of State and semi-government borrowings were excluded from its control. In May 1985, however, the Commonwealth and States agreed to bring all borrowings by Commonwealth, State and local authorities, government-owned companies and trusts within voluntarily agreed limits, while increasing the flexibility of authorities to borrow in Australia and overseas in ways best suited to their requirements.

The *Premiers' Conference* is usually held with a meeting of the Loan Council. This enables Premiers and Federal Ministers to discuss Commonwealth financial assistance to the States and other common problems.

A *National Debt Sinking Fund*, supervised by the National Deb Commission, has been established to reduce the national debt and repa loans as they become due. The Federal and State Governments contribu to this fund in agreed proportions. The Federal Government not on helps to pay the States' debts but also contributes a fixed sum towa the cost of their annual liability for interest charges.

Social Security

One of the tasks of government that has become increasingly important in recent years is the provision of social security. Through its government at Federal, State and local levels, the Australian community accepts responsibility to help and care for those of its citizens who are unable to look after themselves adequately or who require assistance at times of personal misfortune or sudden need. Pensions for the aged, widowed, disabled and sole parents, and payments to the sick and unemployed, are no longer regarded as a form of charity but as benefits a civilised community has an obligation to provide.

Australia was a pioneer of social security at the beginning of this century. New South Wales and Victoria introduced aged pensions in 1901, seven years before Britain did, and they were followed by Queensland in 1908. The Constitution in 1901 gave the Federal Government specific powers to provide age and invalid pensions, but the Commonwealth did not begin to pay age pensions until 1909 and invalid pensions until 1910, superseding the State schemes. In 1912, the Commonwealth introduced a system of maternity allowances.

Between the two world wars, some of the States were more active in developing social security, but since 1939 the Commonwealth has been predominant in this field. Even before the Commonwealth was granted more extensive powers over social security when the Constitution was amended in 1946 by referendum, Federal social security expanded tremendously. Child endowment (now called family allowances), funeral benefits for pensioners, allowances to dependants of invalid pensioners, unemployment and sickness benefits were introduced between 1941 and 1945. A new development since the war was government-subsidised schemes for hospital, medical and pharmaceutical benefits.

State governments are still responsible for general hospitals, the care f the mentally ill and handicapped, and for children's welfare, although me of these services are largely financed from Federal funds. Local ernment councils may provide such services as baby health centres, ergartens, emergency home help and elderly citizens' clubs.

e Federal Government has a special responsibility to care for the d women who served in the armed forces in time of war, and for ndants of deceased ex-servicemen. War and service pensions and nge of repatriation benefits are provided through the Veterans' partment.

hitlam Labor Government (1972–75) introduced a national eme (Medibank) under which all who could afford to do so ed according to their income, and everyone was eligible for free t in public hospitals and community health centres, and for rebates for private medical treatment. It also had plans for a national superannuation scheme and a national compensation and rehabilitation scheme.

The Liberal–NCP Government elected in 1975 retreated from the idea of such Government-sponsored schemes covering all citizens. Opposed to the concept of the 'welfare state' for political and financial reasons, it believed that people, so far as possible, should be encouraged to take responsibility for their own well-being. It argued that the financial burden on the taxpayer and dependence on government aid should be reduced and that priority should be given to helping the neediest.

Accordingly, by 1981 only pensioners, the unemployed and other low-income earners were eligible for free hospital and medical treatment. Other people had to insure privately for health care or pay hospital and medical bills in full. The Hawke Labor Government elected in 1983 restored the Medibank concept, with the new name of Medicare, which is partly financed by a 1.4 per cent surcharge on personal income tax.

Some economists and parliamentarians favour the concept of a 'negative income tax' as a means of reducing poverty. The basic assumption behind this is that everyone is entitled to a minimum level of income. People above this level would pay income tax; those who, for whatever reason, fall below it, would receive cash benefits. Advocates of this idea argued that it would simplify the complex structure of social welfare and make the most effective use of welfare funds by reducing the cost of administering a multitude of schemes. Critics reply that many people dependent on welfare programmes are not only short of money but also need help to cope with their problems or disabilities. Others argue that a guaranteed minimum income would reduce the incentive to look for work.

By the 1990s, even under a Labor Government, the trend was again towards stricter criteria and tougher income and assets tests for pensions and benefits. Because of a rising proportion of retired people in the community and because people are living longer, government policy is to make employees save for their retirement through superannuation schemes, funded through a rising scale of contributions by or levies on employers (in lieu of wage rises) and later to be supplemented by deductions from wage-earners' pay. The coalition parties also favour the switch of emphasis from pensions paid from taxation to fully funded superannuation to reduce the demand for and level of dependence on social security payments. However, they prefer incentives for voluntary superannuation rather than compulsory contributions.

For further thought

- What sort of tasks of government can be better done by statutory bodies than by government departments, and why?
- What is the case for and against privatisation of government business enterprises?
- Does the Australian tax system rely too heavily on income tax paid by wage-earners? What are the arguments for and against a goods and services tax?
- When is it better to finance public works from loans rather than from revenue?
- Which is preferable and why: national health and welfare under which everyone contributes according to their means and benefits according to their needs, or a system under which people are basically responsible for themselves and government aid is confined to the really needy?
- What are the advantages of a national superannuation scheme over pensions paid from taxation?

9

FEDERALISM

Australia, as we have seen, had a federal structure of government in which power is shared between the Commonwealth and the States. The formal division is set out in the Commonwealth Constitution. In theory, the two areas of government should be autonomous and complementary. In practice, they are inter-dependent and overlapping. The system makes for 'weak' government. The Federal Government is limited in its powers, although it has extended its authority and influence. The States are limited in their financial resources. The system requires a fair degree of cooperation to work smoothly, but because of differences in interests and political outlook this is often difficult to achieve.

(The third tier—local government—cannot be considered independent. It is controlled by the States.)

Since Federation, both Federal and State Governments have taken on more and more responsibilities, especially in economic policy, social welfare, foreign affairs, defence and development. But the scope, influence and importance of the Federal Government, although its powers are limited by the Constitution, have grown more than those of the States.

Some people would say that this is a natural outcome of Australia's growing maturity as a nation. Australians increasingly have come to expect government to decide, guide and provide in the interests of the whole or sections of the community. Often these expectations call for action on a national scale, particularly in times of war or economic troubles, and mostly only the national Government has the resources to respond. But other people believe that the Federal Government is becoming too powerful and pervasive and that the balance between the Commonwealth and the States should be restored. Those who favour the predominance of the national Government are often called 'centralists', while those who assert 'State rights' may be called 'federalists'. Some people, and some political leaders, would like the activities of all levels of government to be reduced and leave more room for private enterprise and individual responsibility.

The power of the Federal Government has increased through:

1 constitutional amendment by referendum or reference;
2 judicial interpretation of the Constitution by the High Court;
3 expanded use by the Federal Government of its existing powers;
4 use of its 'power of the purse'; and
5 cooperative federalism.

The trend to centralism has been a constant source of tension and conflict between the Commonwealth and States, and sometimes among the States themselves. Most of the arguments have been over money, but there have been other disagreements, such as over Aboriginal affairs, protection of the environment, and offshore mineral rights.

CHANGING THE CONSTITUTION

The Australian Constitution, like many other written constitutions setting out 'ground rules' of government, is extremely difficult to change. There are three ways in which it may be formally amended or in which additional powers may be transferred to the Federal Government.

1 As the original Constitution was in the form of an Act of the British Parliament, it could, in theory, be changed by the British Parliament. But this has never happened, and almost certainly never will happen.

2 In practice, the Constitution may be altered only with the consent of the Australian people, given in a *referendum*. Three steps are necessary:

a A Bill to amend the Constitution must be passed by an absolute majority of both Houses of Parliament—that is, by more than half the membership of each House, not just half the number in attendance at the time. If the Senate dissents, the Bill may be passed a second time by the House of Representatives after an interval of three months.

b Then, no sooner than two months and no later than six months after the Bill is passed, the proposal must be referred to the electors in the form of a question to which they are asked to vote *Yes* or *No*. To succeed, the proposal must be approved by—

i a majority of the electors voting in at least four of the six States, and

ii a majority of all electors voting, including those in the two mainland Territories. For amendments to alter the federal representation or the boundaries of a State, the approval of a majority of electors is required in the State concerned.

c Finally, if these requirements are met the proposed law, like any other, must be presented to the Governor-General for the Royal Assent, which is normally given as a matter of course.

The Australian people have not been eager to make changes in the Constitution. In ninety-two years since Federation, forty-two proposals (some covering more than one point) were submitted to referendums on eighteen occasions. Only eight proposals were accepted, three of them in 1977. The most important proposal accepted was in 1946 when the people agreed to let the Federal Government provide hospital and medical benefits and a number of other social services. On that occasion, all six States and more than fifty-four per cent of the electors voted in favour. Other successful amendments were in 1906, when some minor changes were made in the procedure for electing Senators; in 1910, when the Commonwealth was enabled to take over State debts; in 1928, concerning financial agreements between the Commonwealth and the States; and in 1967, to include Aboriginal people in censuses and to give the Federal Government power to legislate on Aboriginal affairs.

In May 1977, Australian voters approved three out of four referendum proposals: to ensure that a casual vacancy in the Senate is filled by a person of the same political party, and for the balance of his or her term; to allow electors in the Territories to vote in constitutional referendums; and to provide for retiring ages of Federal judges. The fourth proposal,

REFERENDUMS CARRIED			
Subject	Date of referendum	States in which majority of voters were in favour	Percentage of voters in favour
Senate elections	Dec. 1906	All	82.65
State debts	Apr. 1910	All except NSW	54.95
State debts	Nov. 1928	All	74.30
Social services	Sep. 1946	All	54.39
Aboriginal census	May 1967	All	90.77
Senate casual vacancies	May 1977	All	73.32
Referendums —Territories	May 1977	All	77.72
Retirement of judges	May 1977	All	80.10

REFERENDUMS DEFEATED

Subject	Date of referendum	States in which majority of voters were in favour	Percentage of voters in favour
Finance	Apr. 1910	Qld, WA, Tas	49.04
Legislative powers	Apr. 1911	WA	39.42
Monopolies	Apr. 1911	WA	39.89
Trade and commerce	May 1913	Qld, WA, SA	49.38
Corporations	May 1913	Qld, WA, SA	49.33
Industrial matters	May 1913	Qld, WA, SA	49.33
Railway disputes	May 1913	Qld, WA, SA	49.13
Trusts	May 1913	Qld, WA, SA	49.78
Nationalisation of monopolies	May 1913	Qld, WA, SA	49.33
Legislative powers	Dec. 1919	Vic., Qld, WA	49.65
Nationalisation of monopolies	Dec. 1919	Vic., Qld, WA	48.64
Industry and commerce	Sep. 1926	NSW, Qld	43.50
Essential services	Sep. 1926	NSW, Qld	42.80
Aviation	Mar. 1937	Vic., Qld	53.56
Marketing	Mar. 1937	None	36.26
Post-war reconstruction and democratic rights	Aug. 1944	WA, SA	45.99
Organised marketing of primary products	Sep. 1946	NSW, Vic., WA	50.57
Industrial employment	Sep. 1946	NSW, Vic., WA	40.66
Rents and prices	May 1948	None	40.66
Powers to deal with communists and communism	Sep. 1951	Qld, WA, Tas	49.44
Parliament	May 1957	NSW	40.25
Prices	Dec. 1973	None	43.81
Incomes	Dec. 1973	None	34.42
Terms of Senators	May 1974	NSW	48.30
Mode of altering the Constitution	May 1974	NSW	47.99
Democratic elections	May 1974	NSW	47.20
Local government bodies	May 1974	NSW	46.85
Simultaneous elections	May 1977	NSW, Vic., SA	62.22
Terms of Senators	Dec. 1984	NSW, Vic.	48.21
Interchange of powers	Dec. 1984	None	43.91
Parliamentary terms	Sep. 1988	None	32.92
Fair elections	Sep. 1988	None	37.60
Local government	Sep. 1988	None	33.62
Rights and freedoms	Sep. 1988	None	30.79

to ensure that Senate elections are held at the same time as those for the House of Representatives, was favoured by about sixty-two per cent of all voters but was defeated because it was opposed by a small majority in three States.

Voters have been particularly reluctant to entrust the Federal Government with greater or exclusive powers over a range of economic and industrial affairs, including control over incomes, prices, rents, corporations, employment, labour disputes and marketing of primary products. One of the most controversial referendums was in 1951 when the Menzies Government sought power to ban the Communist Party. This was narrowly defeated. Politically, no referendum is likely to succeed unless it is actively supported by both major political parties in Federal Parliament and most of the States.

There have been three other Federal referendums which were not to alter the Constitution. Two sought approval for conscription for overseas military service during the First World War, and both were rejected. The other was the poll in 1977 for a national song. Voting was preferential as for the House of Representatives, and after the distribution of preferences, 'Advance Australia Fair' became the national song.

Why have so many referendum proposals been rejected? Often the vote has been very close. Several repeatedly unsuccessful attempts to give the Commonwealth increased powers over trade, commerce, monopolies and employment were approved by a majority of electors in three States and by more than forty-nine per cent of all voters. Four proposals were approved by a majority of all voters but not by a majority of States. Probably many people felt that the Federal Government was not to be trusted with extra powers; others might have simply not understood or cared about the issues involved, and decided to play safe by voting No; others again might have been confused by divisions between the political parties over the proposals.

Apart from the complexity of the whole referendum procedure, another aspect may be seen as unsatisfactory. It is that the initiative for a federal referendum must come from the Commonwealth: there is no way the States can move for an amendment of the Constitution without a Bill first being passed by Federal Parliament.

3   The scope of Federal powers can also be increased by one or more of the States *referring* any of their powers to the Commonwealth, under Section 51 (xxxvii) of the Constitution. Tasmania has transferred to the Commonwealth powers over civil aviation in that State, but generally the States have been reluctant to yield powers to Canberra. Towards the end of the Second World War, the Federal Government asked the States to refer fourteen powers thought to be necessary for postwar reconstruction, but could not persuade them all to agree. In 1973, the Whitlam Labor

Form C   (To be initialled on back by
Issuing Officer before issue)

Commonwealth of Australia

POSTAL BALLOT-PAPERS

STATE OF VICTORIA

Referendums on Proposed Constitution Alterations

DIRECTIONS TO VOTER

Write "YES" or "NO" in the space provided opposite each of the questions set out below.

1. An Act to change the terms of senators so that they are no longer of fixed duration and to provide that Senate elections and House of Representatives elections are always held on the same day.

DO YOU APPROVE this proposed alteration?

2. An Act to enable the Commonwealth and the States voluntarily to refer powers to each other.

DO YOU APPROVE this proposed alteration?

FURTHER DIRECTIONS: Fold the ballot-paper, place it in the envelope addressed to the Divisional Returning Officer and fasten the envelope.

6217(F1)   F D Atkinson Government Printer Melbourne   R84/404

A postal ballot paper for a Federal referendum.

Government suggested that the States should transfer their powers to control prices and incomes, but their reluctance led the Government to decide instead on a referendum, which failed.

Among the weaknesses of this reference power are the following:

a there is doubt whether States which agree to refer powers can attach conditions or even later revoke the reference;

b powers referred in this way can be exercised only in the State or States which referred them; and

c the Commonwealth has no power to refer any of its powers back to the States.

A referendum proposal in 1984 to enable the Commonwealth and States to refer powers to each other was defeated.

THE HIGH COURT

Attempts to alter or add to the wording of the Constitution have not done a great deal to increase the powers of the Federal Government. More effective have been changes in the *judicial interpretation* of the original wording. The federation founders were not as clear as they might have been when they wrote some parts of the Constitution, and they could not have foreseen the vast changes that have occurred in Australian life over the past ninety-two years. But they did realise that there would be disputes over the meaning of the Constitution. For this reason they set up the High Court. Any private person, organisation or government that believes that Federal Parliament, in passing a law, has gone beyond the powers given to it by the Constitution can challenge that law in the High Court. (The court does not act on its own initiative.) If the court finds that Parliament did not have power to make the law, then the law is declared unconstitutional and has no force.

Since 1901 the court has given more than 500 constitutional decisions and has declared more than eighty laws unconstitutional wholly or in part. Judges at different times have differed in their approach, but, overall, judicial interpretation has done more to increase the scope of Federal power than to lessen it, particularly in the fields of defence, industrial arbitration, and control over business corporations.

Some of the most important disputes over the Constitution have been on the meaning of Section 92. This states: 'On the imposition of uniform duties of customs, trade, commerce and intercourse among the States, whether by means of internal carriage or ocean navigation, shall be absolutely free.' These simple-sounding words were probably intended to mean that once there were uniform Federal customs duties, there should not be any customs barriers between the States. But the High Court, over several decades until 1989, tended to interpret them in a more restrictive way so as to limit the powers of the Federal and State Governments in favour of private enterprise and individual rights. For example, it prevented the Commonwealth from taking over private airlines and banks operating in more than one State. In a watershed case in 1989 (*Cole* v. *Whitfield*), the court brought its interpretation of Section 92 back to what the founding fathers had intended: that the section simply should stop Governments from imposing discriminatory burdens having a protectionist purpose or effect.

Especially since 1970, a majority of judges on the High Court have given decisions which tend to expand the powers of the Commonwealth. In the important *Concrete Pipes* case of 1971, the court gave a broader meaning to the Commonwealth power to regulate trading and financial corporations. This enabled the Federal Government to control monopolies and restrictive trade practices in ways which had been denied in referendums in the first quarter century of federation. In the *Tasmanian Dams* case of 1983, the court liberally interpreted the Commonwealth external affairs power by ruling that Commonwealth obligations under international treaties and conventions gave it the right to override inconsistent State law (in this case, the Tasmanian Government's plan to build a dam for hydro-electricity in a natural wilderness protected by a World Heritage listing). This expanded power might enable the Commonwealth to set national standards in other areas, such as civil, economic and social rights.

In the past five years the High Court has upheld the Federal Government's Corporations Law (regulating companies, formerly a State responsibility) and Racial Discrimination Act. In 1992 it struck down Federal legislation banning political advertising on radio and television, arguing that this was contrary to freedom of expression implied in the Constitution. This decision has led to speculation that the court might in future uphold other freedoms implied, not expressly guaranteed, in the Constitution. In another controversial decision in 1992 arising from the *Mabo* case, the court held that native title to land was not necessarily extinguished by European settlement in 1788. This does not mean that Aborigines and Torres Strait Islanders can successfully claim any land in Australia. Rather, they might be able to make legal claims to land which is not owned by someone else and with which they can prove continuous association. Such title could, however, be extinguished by Federal or State legislation. Some States wish to do so, but could be overruled by Federal law.

EXPANSION OF POWERS

With or without the help of the High Court, the Federal Government has greatly expanded the use of its exclusive and concurrent powers. For instance, its powers to control posts and telegraphs were extended to cover broadcasting and later television. Powers over interstate transport and international treaties were used to control civil aviation. The defence powers were invoked in wartime to justify a great number of controls over economic activities, but most of these controls did not last long after the Second World War.

The Federal Government has also become an increasingly important influence on the economic life of the nation through, for example, its policies on tariff protection of Australian industries; subsidies to rural industries and regulation of marketing of primary products; fixing of wages and conditions through the arbitration system or Accord with the ACTU; varying interest rates through the central banking system; and the immigration programme.

THE POWER OF THE PURSE

The main way in which the importance of the Federal Government has grown is through its *financial powers*. Its financial dominance sprang largely from three sources: its control of most tax revenue, its power to make grants of money to the States on its own terms, and its regulation through the Loan Council of borrowing by the States. The result was that the States could no longer raise enough taxation to meet their expenses and came to depend on the Commonwealth for much of their income. They were also limited in the amounts they could borrow for public works.

The Federal Government now usually collects more than seventy-five per cent of all tax revenues in Australia while State Governments and

local government raise less than twenty-five per cent. (The proportion was seventy-eight to twenty-two per cent in 1990–91.) Yet the State and local government sector is responsible for fifty per cent of spending on public works, services and administration.

Since its foundation, the Federal Government has had the sole right to collect customs and excise duties, and the High Court has extended this to include sales tax. Until the middle of the Second World War, the Commonwealth and States imposed separate income taxes. In 1942 the Federal Government decided it would collect all income tax and give each State a share. Some States challenged this uniform taxation in the High Court, but it has continued.

This system has been the cause of continual wrangling, usually at the annual Premiers' Conferences. A former Victorian Premier recently described these meetings as 'a ritual of farce and bullying'. The Commonwealth decides how much it will raise in income tax and how much it will keep for its own needs. The States have to be content with what the Commonwealth is willing to give them. In recent years, the Federal Government has cut back on its tax reimbursements (now called revenue assistance grants) to the States for economic reasons, forcing the States, so they complain, to reduce their spending more drastically than the Commonwealth has cut its own spending.

There is also strife over how the Federal grants should be shared among the States. Although the formula recommended by the Grants Commission changes from time to time, New South Wales and Victoria have long had to subsidise the financially weaker States. This is called 'horizontal fiscal equalisation' and is intended to ensure an equality in the level and quality of State services throughout Australia. The two big States now argue that Queensland and Western Australia can afford to be more self-sufficient and need less money from the Commonwealth. New South Wales and Victoria would be better off if they could again raise (and keep) their own income tax (or, better still, get the Commonwealth to collect for them). Constitutionally they could do so, but the political and practical difficulties are too great, especially if the Commonwealth refuses to reduce its income tax accordingly.

Most of the Federal grants are for general revenue purposes; the States themselves can decide how to use the money. But a significant proportion of Federal payments take the form of specific purpose grants; the Commonwealth lays down for what and how this money is to be spent by the States. Some Federal Governments—especially the Whitlam Government (1972–75)—have used this method to subsidise or extend control over education, housing, highways, transport, irrigation and conservation. All were originally areas of sole State responsibility. Some of these grants were given on quite detailed conditions which some State

Governments deeply resented. However, they had little choice but to accept such tied grants, because they needed the money, while continuing to demand the freedom to determine their own priorities without Federal directives.

Another source of irritation in Federal–State financial relations has arisen from the operation of the Loan Council, which the Federal Government has used to control the financing of State public works for reasons of economic policy. Although some States have run up substantial debt, they believe that they should not be restricted by the Federal Government in the amounts they may borrow for their own purposes.

Since 1975 Federal–State relations have had their ups and downs. The Fraser Liberal–NCP Government (1975–83), with the declared aim of making the States less dependent on Federal funds, legislated to allow the States to raise additional revenue by levying a surcharge on income tax. But as the Commonwealth would not reduce its level of taxation, no State was willing to take the unpopular step of imposing extra tax on its residents.

The Hawke Labor Government elected in 1983 accepted in modified form a Grants Commission recommendation to give New South Wales and Victoria a fairer share of Federal funds, and eased some of the Loan Council restrictions on State borrowings. It also floated an idea in 1990 for shared national income tax, that is, the right of the States to receive an agreed component of the personal income tax collected from their residents by the Commonwealth. This proposal to give the States greater financial independence won little political or popular support, and was not taken up.

Since Paul Keating became Prime Minister in 1991, Federal–State relations have become cooler. Mr Keating argues that Australia needs strong central government to achieve essential national goals and to manage efficiently a complex modern economy. He does not believe that the States should be entrusted with more powers or money.

COOPERATIVE FEDERALISM

The Federal and State Governments have agreed to work together in a number of areas and ways where coordination of policies, or uniform legislation, or joint action is desirable, or where the Federal Government provides funds for State activities. Some States have appointed a Minister with a special responsibility for Federal Affairs.

Among the ways in which the Federal and State Governments co-operate are:

1 *Councils and conferences* of Ministers or officials. Premiers' Conferences and the Loan Council provide annual or more frequent opportunities for Federal and State leaders to discuss economic problems and Federal–State financial arrangements. Meetings for other purposes now come under the title of Council of Australian Governments. The Agricultural Council, of relevant Federal and State Ministers, has met regularly since 1934 to coordinate agricultural policies. New Zealand now is also represented on this council, and on the Minerals and Energy Council. There are similar councils or standing committees of Attorneys-General and Ministers for Consumer Affairs, Cultural Affairs, Education, Health, Housing, Industry and Technology, Sport and Recreation, Tourism, and Transport. Some portfolios also have advisory councils of senior Federal and State officials.

2 *Uniform legislation.* Federal and State Governments may agree to pass parallel legislation on a subject, such as company law or hire-purchase. In other cases, the Commonwealth, if the Constitution permits, may pass legislation which supersedes State law, such as on marriage and divorce. Federal and State Ministers have long sought agreement on uniform traffic laws.

3 *Joint bodies.* The Joint Coal Board is an example of cooperation where neither the Federal nor State Government had the sole or sufficient power to control the coal industry in New South Wales. Other joint bodies (some with outside representatives as well) include the National Health and Medical Research Council, the Snowy Mountains Council, the National Rail Corporation and the Australian Tourist Commission.

4 *Advisory bodies.* These are appointed by the Federal Government to advise on the allocation of grants for purposes largely under State administration. They include the Schools Council and Higher Education Council of the National Board of Employment, Education and Training (formerly the Schools Commission and Tertiary Education Commission).

5 *Advisory Council for Inter-government Relations.* This body was established in 1976 to investigate and advise on problems of inter-government relations and foster a cooperative approach. It consists of twenty-four members and an observer appointed by Federal, State, Territory and local governments. Its main work so far has been to study the costs and benefits of staff exchange programmes among the three tiers of government, and to undertake detailed research into local government.

CONSTITUTIONAL REFORM

Many Australians believe that the Constitution ought to be reviewed and brought up to date to meet the needs of a society that has vastly changed since the document was drafted nearly a century ago. It is also clear that the responsibilities and financial resources of the Commonwealth and the States need to be brought into better balance. There have been several initiatives over the past twenty years to examine and revise the Constitution, with little success.

In 1973 Federal and State Governments set up a Constitutional Convention of ninety-six Federal and State members of Parliament and twenty-four representatives of local government and the Northern Territory. It met six times between 1973 and 1985 amid continual political disagreements. It recommended a number of changes but only three proposals to amend the Constitution succeeded at referendum. These were to allow people in the Territories to vote in referendums, to fix a retiring age for Federal judges, and to ensure that a Senator who dies or retires during his or her term is replaced by a member of the same party. Nine other referendums were defeated.

In 1985 the Federal Labor Government appointed a six-member Constitution Commission to draw up a new Constitution in time for Australia's Bicentenary in 1988. It issued a comprehensive report but there was little support for its adoption. The Federal Government decided to put four questions to referendum in 1986 but because of political controversy over their wording and suspicion of the Government's motives, none gained a majority in any State.

In 1991, a Constitutional Centenary Foundation was formed under the chairmanship of a former Governor-General and High Court judge, Sir Ninian Stephen. Its role is to encourage public education and debate about the Constitution, rather than propose any specific changes, in the lead up to the centenary of Federation on 1 January 2001.

By 1993 interest in constitutional reform had become diverted into the debate pushed by the Keating Government over whether Australia should become a republic.

For further thought

- In what ways, if any, is the Constitution too narrow and rigid to allow the Federal Government to keep pace with changes in the modern world and to fulfil the needs of a developing country?
- It is generally agreed that the Federal Government should have a large measure of control over the Australian economy. Should the Federal Government be given greater financial powers—such as over wages, interest rates, rents, prices, hire purchase and investment—to strengthen its economic policy?
- The Victorian Government has complained that under uniform taxation Victorians pay too much to the Commonwealth and get too

little back. Is this a good reason for abolishing uniform taxation, or is it in the national interest that the wealthier States help to pay for the development of the less fortunate States?

- Should the Constitution include a Bill of Rights?

10

THE REPUBLICAN DEBATE

Sooner or later—perhaps before the turn of the century—Australians will be asked whether the nation should end its links with the monarchy and become a republic. Like any other Constitutional change, such a move would have to be approved by referendum in the procedure already described. Public support for the idea, as measured by opinion polls, has been growing, and the Federal Labor Government led by Paul Keating is committed to it. However, opinion is sharply divided. Support for republicanism is strongest among younger people, citizens of non-British ancestry, city dwellers, and those on the Left of politics. Support for the monarchy is strongest among older people, those of British (but not Irish) ancestry, country people, and those of conservative persuasion. The Labor Party is in favour of a republic, Liberal Party opinion is divided but mostly against it, and the National Party is firmly for the monarchy.

Both sides put forward both philosophical, sentimental and practical arguments. Monarchists see the Queen of Australia as an enduring and gracious symbol of national unity above the hurly-burly of political strife, and perhaps the ultimate guardian of the nation's democratic institutions. They point out that Australia is for all intents and purposes a fully independent nation, quite free of any colonial ties or subordination, and that the Governor-General (and Governors in the States) are the de facto heads of state under the Commonwealth and State Constitution and its laws. They believe that there is no compelling need for change, and suspect that the Keating Government has a political agenda—to divide the Opposition and divert attention from economic problems—in pushing for a republic.

Republicans argue that the concept of a shared, hereditary, normally absentee monarchy—regardless of any practical advantages or lack of

THERE'S GOING TO BE ANOTHER DIVORCE IN THE FAMILY ... AUSTRALIA WANTS ONE

internal interference—is an illogical anachronism for a mature, independent and multicultural country such as Australia. They point out that Britain is now part of the European Community and contend that the Queen could have conflicts of interest in being head of state of several realms with differing national interests. A break with the monarchy, they say, need not mean any significant change in the way we are governed but simply recognise the underlying reality behind the royal 'myth'.

WHAT KIND OF REPUBLIC?

If Australia is to adopt a republican Constitution, the first question to be answered is 'what kind of republic?' The world offers a range of models, but the main division is between republics like the United States, where the President is both the head of state and the head of government or chief executive, and those, such as Germany, where the head of state is mainly a ceremonial figurehead and the head of government is the Prime Minister (or Chancellor in Germany). France has an intermediate system: a President with strong executive powers and a Prime Minister responsible to Parliament.

The republican consensus in Australia is that we should retain the Westminster system of responsible government and that the presidency (whatever it is called) should be largely a ceremonial post with more or less the formal and reserve powers at present exercised by the Governor-General. Australia would also be likely to remain a Federation, although some people would like to abolish States in favour of a strong national government with subordinate regional administrations.

If this model is chosen, then there is a choice between the so-called 'minimalist' and 'maximalist' positions. The minimalists say that little more would be necessary than to remove all references to the Queen in the Constitution and other laws, and substitute that of the Governor-General, who would simply have the same powers and duties that he has now. The main argument for this formula is that it would cause the least disturbance to our system of government and would likely be the most acceptable to the electorate. Maximalists contend that if we are to have a new Constitution, then we may as well make the most of it and fashion it to meet the needs and wishes of contemporary society. Such a new Constitution could, for example, entrench a Bill of Rights, limit the power of the Senate to obstruct the House of Representatives, and provide for a better balance of revenue resources and responsibilities between the Commonwealth and States (or abolish the States altogether). However, the more changes that are proposed, the greater the opposition is likely to be, and the harder it would be to gain popular support.

HOW TO CHOOSE THE HEAD OF STATE?

Even if the minimalist position—apparently favoured by the Keating Government—is favoured, further questions arise. What should the head of state be called—Governor-General, President, or some other title? More importantly, how should he or she be chosen?

There are broadly four options:

1 Appointment by the Federal Government, with or without consulting the Opposition. This is how the Governor-General is chosen now, except that the Queen makes the formal appointment.
2 Appointment on the recommendation of an electoral college (perhaps including State representatives) or a panel of eminent persons (such as the Prime Minister, Opposition Leader and Chief Justice).
3 Election by Federal Parliament, but if so, how?—by the two Houses sitting separately or jointly? or by simple or two-thirds majority?
4 Direct election by the people. This might appear to be the most democratic method, but it raises the problem of how to resolve possible conflicts between a popularly elected President and a Prime Minister or Government with a parliamentary majority—each claiming a popular mandate.

Other questions to be answered are what term the President should serve, what reserve powers the President should have (would they be spelled out in the Constitution or left to convention?), and in what circumstances and how the President could be removed.

What about the States?

Another difficult question stems from the Federal system. Not only the Commonwealth Constitution but also the State Constitutions would have to be changed. The Constitutions of the States can be amended by their Parliaments (some require a two-thirds majority) without the need for a referendum. What would happen if the Commonwealth became a republic but one or more of the States chose not to do so? Would the Governor of such a State again be appointed by and responsible to the Queen of Great Britain, as there would no longer be a Queen of Australia?

The Keating Federal Government has appointed a Republic Advisory Committee, headed by a lawyer and merchant banker, Mr Malcolm Turnbull, to examine these issues and foster public discussion.

The Australian flag

A related but separate question is whether Australia should adopt a national flag of a different design. This is also a very emotional issue. It would not require a Constitutional amendment but could be put to a popular vote by plebiscite. People who want a change generally object to the Union Jack in the top corner and would prefer a more distinctive design that does not look like any other. Those who are opposed to any change tend to have a strong sentimental attachment to the present flag and argue that the Union Jack represents part of Australia's history. If Australia became a republic, there would probably be greater support for a new flag to mark the occasion. However, Australia could, like Canada, opt for a new flag without breaking its links with the monarchy.

For further thought

- Why do you think Australia should—or should not—become a republic?
- What are the difficulties in the way of such a step?
- If there were to be a change, what kind of republic should be considered, and how should the head of state be chosen?
- What is the case for and against adopting a new Australian flag? What alternative design would you favour?

CHAPTER

11

LOCAL GOVERNMENT

Soon after his arrival in the young colony of New South Wales, Governor Bourke in 1832 remarked that the time seemed ripe for inhabitants of Sydney

> to administer to their own convenience and comfort, by providing, by means of a body elected among themselves, for the repairing, cleansing and lighting the streets, the construction of flagged footpaths and the introduction of water into public fountains and private houses. These useful objects may be obtained at no great cost by a rate levied on houses, according to their estimated value, and collected and appropriated by commissioners elected annually by the ratepayers.

Governor Bourke's suggestion of a system of local government, modelled on that of England, aroused little enthusiasm among the residents of Sydney. The colonists were well aware of the need for local services, but strongly objected to having to pay for them. Ten years passed before Sydney elected its first city corporation and Melbourne its town council. At the same time, foundations were laid, not very successfully at first, for a system of district councils in New South Wales.

From these beginnings, local government slowly spread over most of Australia. Apart from the Australian Capital Territory and some sparsely populated outback areas, practically the whole country is divided into nearly 900 local government areas. The number is likely to decrease as some States, notably Victoria, have plans to amalgamate local councils in inner metropolitan and large urban areas, and in rural areas with too few people or not enough revenue.

Local government areas are of four main types:

1 small, densely populated suburban units in mostly large metropolitan cities;

2 independent urban centres;

3 large rural units where the population is spread over a wide area. In population, local government areas range from as few as a thousand people to more than 150 000;

4 areas in the Northern Territory and Queensland controlled by Aboriginal communities with their own councils.

The urban units are called cities or municipalities in New South Wales; cities, towns or boroughs in Victoria; cities or towns in Queensland and Western Australia; and cities and corporate towns in South Australia. The rural units are known as shires in all mainland States except South Australia, where they are known as district council areas. In Tasmania, six urban areas are now incorporated as cities and the rest of the State is divided into forty municipalities. In most States, local government areas are divided into wards (in urban areas) or ridings (in shires). Local government in the Northern Territory is described in the chapter on Territories.

THE COUNCILS

Local government units in all States are controlled by elected councils. Methods of election vary from State to State. Originally, only property owners who paid rates could vote. In some States, people with property of a high rateable value had multiple votes. Plural voting in the same council election is now allowed only in Western Australia, but, in all States except Queensland, ratepayers may also vote in areas where they own property other than where they live. Later, the franchise in all States was extended to occupiers of property, and perhaps ex-servicemen and women. Now, in all States except Western Australia and Tasmania, anyone who is on the State or Federal electoral roll is also entitled to vote in local council elections. South Australia has gone further by allowing residents who are not Australian citizens to vote in local elections.

NEW SOUTH WALES

Most municipalities and shires have combined in groups to form *country councils* to provide special services that can be organised more efficiently and economically over a large area, such as electricity and water supply. They are really joint committees elected from and by local councils in adjoining areas. Some shires have subordinate *urban areas* to provide for the special needs of small towns within a mainly rural district. An area can become a *municipality* if it has a distinct character and entity as a centre of population of at least 150 000, or if it is an independent centre with a population of at least 25 000.

Councils are elected for four years by residents on the State electoral roll. Voting is compulsory. Proportional representation is used in wards with three or more seats; elsewhere, the system is preferential. Members of urban councils are called councillors. The lord mayors of Sydney, Newcastle and Parramatta and the mayors of urban (municipal and city) councils are elected by popular vote. Mayors of shires (formerly shire presidents) are mostly elected by councillors but may be popularly elected if a council so chooses.

VICTORIA

Victoria had 205 local government councils in mid-1993, more than any other State. The State Government intends to reduce the number to about a hundred. It has begun by merging six former councils and taking in parts of two shires to form the Greater Geelong City Council. A *shire* may be any size and population. A *borough* must be substantially urban in character and have a population of at least 4000. It can become a *town* if it has 5000 or more inhabitants, or a *city* when its population reaches 10 000.

Councils are elected for three years, one-third of councillors retiring at each annual election. Voting by residents on the State electoral roll is compulsory. The preferential system is used. The lord mayor of Melbourne, mayors of cities, towns and boroughs, and shire presidents are all elected by councillors.

QUEENSLAND

There are no special requirements before an urban area may be proclaimed as a town or city, but the size and concentration of population are taken into account. The whole of Brisbane is administered by a single city council.

Councils are elected for three years by all persons on the State electoral roll. Voting is compulsory. In many shires, voting is entirely by post. In Brisbane, the preferential voting system is used. In other areas, the required number of candidates winning the greatest number of votes are elected, each elector having as many votes as the number of candidates to be elected. Mayors and shire chairpersons are elected by the voters. So, now, is the lord mayor of Brisbane.

South Australia

A district may become a *corporate town* if it is settled mainly as a residential, business or industrial centre and is able to support itself financially. A municipality can become a *city* when it has a population of 10 000 (in the country) or 15 000 (in the metropolitan area of Adelaide).

Councils are elected for two years, half the councillors retiring each year. Voting is voluntary by the preferential system. All residents, even if they are not Australian citizens, may vote. The lord mayor of Adelaide and all mayors are elected by the voters, but shire presidents are elected by the councillors. In South Australia only, 'aldermen' are additional councillors of experience elected for the whole area, not for wards.

Western Australia

There are no special requirements for shires and towns. A *city* must meet these three tests:

1 a population of 20 000 if in the country or 30 000 in the metropolitan area for at least three years;
2 a gross revenue from all sources of $200 000 a year in this period; and
3 a clearly distinguishable centre of population, with a distinct and sufficient civic centre and sufficient residential, commercial, industrial and cultural facilities.

Councils are elected for three years, one-third retiring at each annual election. Voting is voluntary and restricted to owners and occupiers of property who are Australian citizens (or British subjects). The preferential system is used. People who pay rates above a certain level may have two votes in the same area. Mayors are usually elected by the voters and shire presidents by the councillors, but councils may choose the opposite system if they wish.

Tasmania

The State is divided into forty municipalities and six cities (Hobart, Launceston, Glenorchy, Devonport, Burnie and Clarence). Urban areas may be declared towns, but these are not administrative areas. Before a municipality can petition for a town to become a city, it must have had, for the five previous years, an average population of not less than 20 000.

Councils are elected for three years, one-third of councillors retiring at each annual election. Voting is voluntary and restricted to owners or occupiers who are Australian citizens (or British subjects). Alien owners or occupiers may, however, have a qualified elector vote on their behalf. The chairperson of a municipal council is called a warden and is elected by the council. The lord mayor of Hobart is directly elected by the voters. The mayors of the other cities may be directly elected by the voters or by the council.

General

Council members, except the 'aldermen' of Brisbane City Council, are not paid salaries, but they may receive allowances. New South Wales councils may pay councillors a fee for each meeting they attend. Mayors usually receive an entertainment allowance.

In some States, Governments have used their powers to suspend certain councils and replace them temporarily with appointed commissioners or administrators. This happened to Sydney City Council in 1927 and 1967, and to the Melbourne City Council in 1981 and 1993.

Political parties are generally not as active in local government as they are in State and Federal government. The Liberal and National Parties usually do not endorse candidates for local elections, but the Labor Party does so in mostly metropolitan areas where it has strong electoral support. Non-Labor councillors may style themselves 'Independents'. In some municipalities, councillors may divide into factions representing business interests or residents' groups.

THE WORK OF LOCAL GOVERNMENT

The councils have been given their powers by State Governments. Their duties are laid down by Acts of Parliament. Councils are *required* to deal with certain matters and *allowed* to deal with certain other matters; beyond these they must not go. An official listing of local government responsibilities in 1975 identified 134 services and functions provided by local government in at least one State. Only twenty-two of these were mandatory (required by the State Government) and none was mandatory in every State. Since then, there have been changes in every State, but it remains true that what local government does varies considerably from State to State. All States have Departments of Local Government (or a section of a bigger department) to supervise the work of local authorities.

The two main functions of local government are to provide works and services for land and property and to offer amenities and welfare services to the local community. Two further aims could be said to be to help mould the local environment and to encourage people to participate in municipal affairs. As a Royal Commission on Local Government in England (1966–69) put it:

Local government is not to be seen merely as a provider of services. If that were all, it would be right to consider whether some of the services could not be more efficiently provided by other means. The importance of local government lies in the fact that it is the means by which people can provide services for themselves; can take an active and constructive part in the business of government; and can decide for themselves, within the limits of what national policies and local resources allow, what kind of services they want and what kind of environment they prefer.

Works and services to service property include those to:
- Construct and maintain local roads and footpaths.
- Light and sweep streets.
- Collect and dispose of garbage.
- Supply water, electricity and gas.
- Provide sewerage or sanitary services.
- Prepare town planning schemes to control land use, housing and industrial development.
- Issue building permits and enforce building regulations.
- Establish sale yards, abattoirs and markets.
- Supervise car parking.
- Register dogs and impound stray animals.

Amenities and services for the local community include those to:
- Enforce health regulations, control infectious diseases, and supervise food shops and boarding houses.
- Conduct baby health clinics, kindergartens and day care centres.
- Employ social workers and provide home help and community support services for the aged and others in need.
- Establish and maintain parks and gardens, sports grounds, camping reserves and swimming pools.
- Run community and recreation centres, and community transport.
- Provide home units, hostels and shelters for the frail aged, the homeless and others in need.
- Offer counselling, legal aid and advice services to the unemployed, immigrants and others with special problems.
- Establish libraries, museums, art galleries, orchestras and bands.

Not all councils do all of these things, but the trend is towards providing more services for people rather than for property, especially with the increase in funds, some for specific purposes, from State and Federal Government sources. Although the powers of rural and urban councils are much the same, the needs of their communities will naturally differ in some ways. A far-flung, sparsely settled shire will be mainly concerned with building and maintaining a network of local roads. In a city or large town, water supply, sewerage, garbage disposal and street lighting are essentials. How many amenities a council provides depends not only on its income and population but also on how public-spirited the local community is. Where councils are elected by ratepayers, there is often a conflict between those who would like more services to be provided and those who want to keep the rates as low as possible.

Some of the duties of local government are shared with State Government authorities. In Victoria, the Roads Corporation is wholly responsible for State highways, by-pass roads, tourist and forest roads, and shares with local councils the cost of maintaining main roads. The corporation also subsidises councils for work on local roads. Similar arrangements apply in other States. In enforcing health and building regulations, councils work under the supervision of State authorities.

Water supply and sewerage in Sydney and Melbourne are provided by statutory authorities and in Adelaide and Perth by Government departments. In most other cities and towns, these services are provided either by local councils or by water trusts, under the supervision of State water supply departments or authorities (which may construct the necessary storage reservoirs).

Some local government functions have been taken over by State Government authorities. In Victoria, nearly all electricity is now supplied by the State Electricity Commission's state-wide network, and the Gas and Fuel Corporation has absorbed several local gasworks. Most harbours are managed by statutory boards, such as the Port of Melbourne Authority or Maritime Services Board of New South Wales. Brisbane City Council is the only municipal council operating buses.

COUNCIL OFFICERS

The administrative staff of each council is headed by a general manager, town clerk, chief executive, city manager or shire secretary, who also acts as secretary to the council. In Victoria, there must also be a treasurer to keep the council's accounts. The engineer is responsible for road making and other technical activities. Most councils have a health inspector, or share one with a neighbouring council. Councils may also appoint valuers, rate collectors, buildings surveyors, traffic officers and other officials, depending on the extent of the council's activities.

PAYING FOR LOCAL GOVERNMENT

The main source of local government revenue is rates—local taxes paid by the owners or occupiers of private property in the municipality and based on the value of the property. An increasingly important source of funds is Government grants, made mainly for roads and as subsidies for particular projects, such as libraries, baby health centres, swimming pools and public halls. In 1977 the Federal Government introduced a plan to give local government a share, through the State Governments, of income tax revenue. Other revenue includes charges for public works and services (such as for making private roads or for garbage collection), rents for hire of council properties and equipment, profits from business undertakings (such as electricity and gas), and local licences, fees and fines.

In addition, councils may borrow money for large public works, business undertakings or expensive equipment when it is considered wise to spread the costs over several years. The conditions under which councils may raise loans are strictly laid down in the Local Government Acts.

RATES

As rates are a tax on property, the values of all private properties within the municipal area must be determined. A council or Government valuer periodically inspects all properties in the municipality and estimates their value. Federal and State Government properties, educational, religious and charitable institutions are generally exempt from rates.

Basically two methods of valuation for the assessment of rates are used in Australia, although the names and precise definitions vary from State to State. One is based on an estimate of what the property could be sold for if nothing were built on it. The other is based on what the property and everything on it could earn in rent each year. In Victoria and Western Australia, councils have an option of using either system, and in Victoria, a few councils use a mixture of both.

1 a *Land, site, unimproved* or *unimproved capital value* is used by all councils in New South Wales (LV) and Queensland (UCV), most shire councils in Western Australia (UV) and many councils in Victoria and South Australia (SV). It is also generally used to assess State land tax. In simple terms, it means the estimated value of the land without any buildings or other visible 'improvements' on it. Land or site value, however, does include such improvements as underground drains and enhancement of soil fertility.

   b South Australia distinguishes between *capital value* (the amount for which land could be sold) and site value (the amount for which the land could be sold excluding any improvements). Councils may choose either method.

2 a *Net annual value* is an estimate of the yearly rent for which a property, including buildings and other improvements, could be let, less the annual expenses (such as land tax, rates, insurance and repairs)

of maintaining it. This method is used by most councils and by Melbourne Water in Victoria.

b *Assessed annual* or *gross rental value* is the rental value of a property without allowing for expenses. This method is used exclusively in Tasmania (AAV) and by most urban councils in Western Australia (GRV). The New South Wales Metropolitan Water, Sewerage and Drainage Board also uses AAV (nine-tenths of the fair average rental) for its purposes.

It makes little difference to a council which system it uses (or is obliged to use). A council can obtain the same overall revenue from either basic method by adjusting the rate in the dollar. For instance, if a property has a site value of $100 000, a rate of 0.25 cents in the dollar would yield $250 a year. If such a property were assessed to have a net annual value of $20 000, a rate of 1.25 cents in the dollar would also produce $250.

However, the burden could fall differently on various classes of ratepayers. That is why in Victoria, where councils have the option of using either system, there are continual arguments as to which is preferable. Under site valuation, for instance, a vacant block pays rates as high as those for a similar block with a house or shop or factory on it. The main argument for site value or its variations is that owners are encouraged to make full use of their land, or sell it to someone who will. It may also be argued that as local services are available equally to improved and unimproved properties, equal rates should be paid. In Victoria, some councils in newer suburban areas prefer site value to discourage speculators from holding unimproved blocks until the land becomes more developed and therefore their land more valuable.

Net annual value is more closely related to one of the fundamental principles of taxation—ability to pay. Those who favour this system point out that people with expensive properties, whether residential or commercial, are better able to afford higher rates than those who are poorer. Contrary to the claims of the advocates of site value, it is also argued that more highly developed properties tend to demand more services. Against NAV is the argument that thrifty and progressive citizens who improve their properties are 'penalised' by having to pay higher rates.

In New South Wales, some of the disadvantages of land valuation are overcome by councils' levying differential rates for urban and rural land, and residential and non-residential properties. But in Victoria, rates do not discriminate between different types of property. Thus, in a new suburb with many vacant allotments, rating under net annual valuation would fall more heavily on people who had built homes, because they would have to pay more than owners of vacant land, and the rate in the dollar would have to be higher to produce enough revenue for the council. In an older, built-up area with a mixture of valuable and poorer properties, a change to unimproved capital valuation would raise rates paid by the poorer properties and lower those paid by the more expensive ones.

METROPOLITAN AUTHORITIES

More than half of the people of Australia live in the six State capital cities. Over the past sixty or seventy years, the formerly separated suburbs and outlying districts have in each of the bigger capitals been linked into a sprawling metropolis. These cities have become fringed with vast 'dormitory' suburbs, in which people live and from which thousands of them travel each day to the commercial and industrial centre to work or shop.

Brisbane is the only State capital with a single city council for its whole metropolitan area: Greater Brisbane, which came into being as a local government area in 1925, covers 1000 square kilometres. The Brisbane City Council not only does the work formerly done by twenty separate councils, but is also responsible for water supply and sewerage, electricity supply, roads, and the city's buses and ferries.

In the other capitals local government is in the hands of a number of separate councils. Sydney and Melbourne each have about fifty. (The Sydney and Melbourne City Councils administer only the central business area of each metropolis.) Essential services shared by the whole metropolitan area—such as water, sewerage, electricity, gas and public transport—are provided by statutory authorities or Government departments.

Efforts made from time to time to establish Greater Sydney or Greater Melbourne councils have all failed. Opposition from local councils which would lose their powers and privileges, disagreement over the composition of a 'greater city council', reluctance to entrust wide powers to a few people, and fear of party politics in local government affairs—these are among the reasons for the failure of such moves.

As Melbourne and Sydney grew in population and area and as the problems of providing essential services became more and more difficult, people realised the need to control development and to plan for future needs. Metropolitan planning in both cities is the responsibility of a State department.

For further thought

- What services and amenities does your local council provide? Are they adequate?
- If you were a ratepayer, would you be prepared to pay more so that your municipality could have, say, a public library or swimming pool?
- Should local councillors be elected by all citizens or only by ratepayers who have to bear most of the cost of local government?
- Which is the fairer system—net annual valuation, or land or site valuation? Which does your local council use, and why?
- If you live in a capital city, do you think your city would be better served by a greater city council than by numerous suburban councils? What would be the advantages and drawbacks of such a greater city council?
- Should there be a limit to the size of metropolitan areas? If so, how can this be achieved?

12

LAW AND JUSTICE

The law under which we live has not all been made by Acts of Parliament. Much of it is older than Parliament itself. The modern world inherited two great original systems of law, the Roman and the English. Law in Australia is founded on English law. The Common Law of England is the result of a thousand years of growth, based on ancient and unwritten custom and developed, from precedent to precedent, by decisions of the King's judges in particular cases.

Strictly speaking, unenacted law (law that has not been made by Parliament) is divided between 'common law' and 'equity'. Equity is a branch of civil law developed in the Middle Ages in the Courts of Chancery under the jurisdiction of the Chancellor, or 'keeper of the King's conscience'. These courts dealt with certain types of cases for which the old common law court had no remedy, and decisions were based on the judges' sense of fair play or natural justice rather than on strict legal rules. Common law and equity are now administered by the same courts.

Law and justice, in an autocratic form, came to Australia with Governor Phillip in 1788. In 1828, laws in force in England, both common law and statute law, were declared to be law in the colony of New South Wales so far as they could reasonably be applied. The infant colony was given power to adopt this inherited law to local conditions and to make new laws. As other colonies were established or separated, they too were brought under this system.

Law in Australia thus consists of:

1 common law and equity, as declared and developed by decisions of judges in the superior courts of England and Australia;

2 statute law, as enacted by the Parliaments of the States and Common-wealth;
3 subordinate legislation, namely the rules, regulations and bylaws made by governments and public authorities on the authority and within the limits of Acts of Parliament.

The common law is found chiefly in the reported decisions of the courts. It is the legal principle on which a decision is based that is binding; the reasoning by which the judges arrived at their decision is what counts, rather than the words in which the decision is given. Australian courts follow the English system of precedent. Simply stated, this means that a court is bound by decisions of any court superior to it. This will be made clearer when we discuss the system of courts.

Statute law has replaced much of what was formerly common law. When a statute covers all the law on a particular subject, it is called a code. The State criminal law has been codified in Queensland, Western Australia and Tasmania; in other States it remains a mixture of common law and statute law. Statute law is not so flexible as common law, as judges must follow what the statutes say, not the general principles behind them.

A distinction may be made between civil and criminal justice. *Civil justice* is concerned with the rights and obligations of citizens, whether as individuals or corporations, in their relations one with another—such as over the ownership of property, or the fulfilment of a contract, or the payment of a debt. In civil cases, the courts settle disputes, enforce legal rights and duties, and remedy wrongs done by one citizen to another.

Criminal justice is concerned with wrongs committed against the well-being of the community, and the criminal courts punish the wrongdoers. Murder or robbery are more than private wrongs to the individual. They strike at fundamental human values—the right to life and the right to property—that form the basis of civilised society. Society must protect itself and its members against such serious crimes, as well as against lesser forms of anti-social behaviour. Crimes can be roughly classed into four types: offences against the State (such as treason, sabotage, sedition), against the person (murder, manslaughter, assault), against property (theft, burglary, wilful damage), and against public order (vagrancy, drunk and disorderly behaviour, traffic offences).

Suppose that a car knocks down and injures a man crossing the road. The injured man may sue the driver of the car for damages. This is a matter of civil justice: a private citizen seeking redress for a wrong done to him. But the police may also prosecute the motorist for dangerous or drunken driving. That is a matter of criminal justice: society seeking punishment for an offence against the public good.

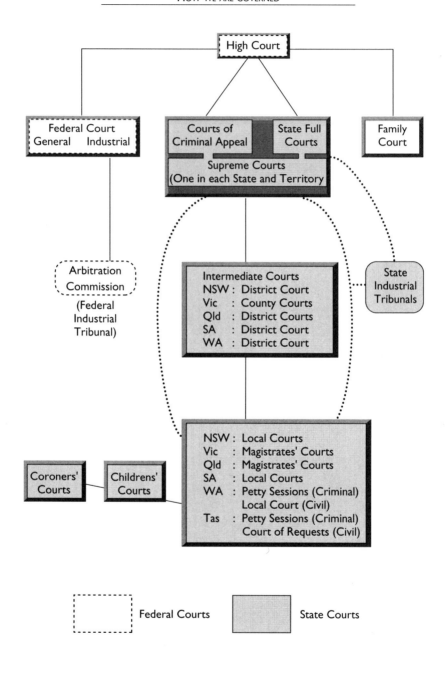

The Australian Judicial System

THE COURTS OF JUSTICE

The administration of justice in Australia is basically a task of State courts. Each State has a Supreme Court and a system of lesser courts, applying both State and Federal laws. The Australian Territories each have their own system of Federal courts. Ranking above the Supreme Courts of the States and Territories is the High Court of Australia, which is a Federal court. Under the High Court are also two specialised Federal courts—the Federal Court and the Family Court. The Federal Court was created in 1976 to absorb the work formerly done by the Industrial Court and the Bankruptcy Court. It also hears appeals from Territory Supreme Courts and from State Supreme Court judges exercising Federal jurisdiction in tax, patents and trade mark matters. The Family Court has been established to take over from the State Supreme Courts the hearing of divorce matters, except in Western Australia, where there is a State Family Court.

MAGISTRATES' COURTS

These are local courts dealing with minor criminal offences and civil cases. They are presided over by paid magistrates, or, in some States, by honorary Justices of the Peace. The administrative work of these courts is done by a clerk of courts. Magistrates, known in some States as stipendiary, police or special magistrates, are usually appointed from the ranks of senior clerks of courts who have passed special examinations. In South Australia and New South Wales, they are chosen from among legal practitioners. Justices of the Peace are men and women of standing in the community who have been granted a Commission of the Peace, an historic appointment dating to the fourteenth century in England. In Victoria, Justices of the Peace no longer sit in court. In New South Wales, Justices of the Peace sit on the bench only in country districts.

The names of the lowest courts vary from State to State. They are called *Magistrates' Courts* in Victoria and Queensland, and *Local Courts* in New South Wales and South Australia. In Western Australia and Tasmania, they are called *Courts of Petty Sessions* in criminal matters, but *Local Courts* and *Courts of Requests* respectively in civil matters.

In their criminal jurisdiction, these courts deal both with minor or summary offences, and hold preliminary inquiries on persons charged with serious crimes to determine whether they should be sent for trial in a higher court. In their civil jurisdiction, the amount of money or value of property involved is limited. In Victoria, the general limit is $5000 for damages claims for personal injury, or $20 000 in most other cases.

A view of a Court of Petty Sessions in Western Australia. The clerk of courts is sitting beneath the magistrate on the bench. The defendant is in the dock on the left. The police prosecutor (standing) is questioning a witness in the box on the right. The defence counsel is seated to the prosecutor's left. The table in front is usually occupied by other lawyers awaiting their client's cases to be heard.

On the same level as Magistrates' Courts are *Coroners' Courts*, which hold inquests into the causes of violent or unnatural deaths, such as drowning, accident or homicide. If the Coroner, who is usually a magistrate, finds someone responsible for the death, he or she may send that person for trial.

All States have special *Children's Courts* to try young offenders. In Victoria, Children's Courts may deal with any offence by persons under seventeen years, except homicide. Proceedings are conducted in a more informal manner than in a normal court, and are not open to the public or press. The special magistrates do their best to understand and help youngsters brought before them. The courts are bound to give first consideration to the child's welfare and reform. Many offenders are released on probation for up to three years, and probation officers are assigned to help and guide them during this period. As a last resort, children may be committed to the care of the Social Welfare Department and sent to an institution, and those aged fifteen or more may be ordered detention in a youth training centre for up to two years.

INTERMEDIATE COURTS

Five States have intermediate courts to deal with criminal and civil matters. They are called the County Court in Victoria and the District Court (or Courts) in New South Wales, Queensland, South Australia and Western Australia.

The more serious crimes, but not the most serious, are tried before a judge and jury in these courts. The courts also hear appeals from Magistrates' Courts. Anyone convicted in a Magistrates' Court may appeal against their conviction or the sentence.

In civil cases, the intermediate courts usually consist of a judge sitting alone, but in some States there may be a jury if the judge thinks it necessary or if either party involved asks for one. In Victoria, jurisdiction is limited to cases where the amount claimed or in dispute is not more than $100 000.

SUPERIOR COURTS

These are the highest courts of each State and Territory, and have jurisdiction over all civil and criminal matters that have not been excluded by statute. The most serious crimes, such as murder, are tried by the Supreme Court (in these cases often called the Criminal Court). The State Supreme Courts each consist of a Chief Justice and several other judges known as puisne (pronounced as 'puny') judges. The Full Court, usually of three judges, hears appeals against decisions of lower courts and of single Supreme Court judges. In criminal appeals the Full Court may be called the Court of Criminal Appeal. The Supreme Courts of the States sit mainly in the capital cities but occasionally go 'on circuit' to other important centres.

THE HIGH COURT

The High Court consists of a Chief Justice and six other justices. It has both appellate jurisdiction (to hear appeals) and original jurisdiction (to hear cases directly, not on appeal from lower courts).

Its appellate jurisdiction, exercised by at least three justices, is more important. The High Court is the highest court of appeal in Australia. It may hear appeals arising from its own original jurisdiction, from the Federal Court, and from State or Territorial Supreme Courts (generally only if special leave is granted). In civil matters, the right of appeal is limited to cases involving property of a certain value or important legal principles.

The High Court has original jurisdiction in matters:

1 arising from or involving interpretation of the Federal Constitution;
2 arising from any treaty or international agreement;
3 involving diplomatic representatives of other countries;
4 in which the Federal Government is directly a party;
5 involving a dispute between States or residents of different States; and
6 in trials of certain indictable offences under Federal laws.

Such cases are usually heard by a single Justice, who may also determine appeals on points of law from decisions of some Federal administrative bodies, such as taxation boards of review.

Since mid-1984, an appeal to the High Court requires the court's consent. This limitation was introduced to reduce the court's heavy work load. The court will give leave for an appeal only if it believes the case involves a principle of legal importance.

The court's main seat has moved from Melbourne to Canberra, but occasionally it also sits in Sydney or Melbourne.

THE PRIVY COUNCIL

The High Court now is the final avenue of appeal for all Australian courts. Until the end of 1985, appeals arising from State Supreme Courts could still be made—in limited circumstances—to the Judicial Committee of the Privy Council in London. The Privy Council is the final court of appeal for British Commonwealth countries beyond Britain which still recognise it as such. It comprises English law lords and certain Common-

The full High Court in session in its majestic building in Canberra—an artist's impression.

wealth judges, including judges of the Australian High Court. In 1968, the Australian Government legislated to make the High Court the final arbiter on all matters of Federal jurisdiction. In 1986, by agreement with all the States, the remaining rights of Australians to appeal to the Privy Council were abolished.

CRIMINAL PROCEEDINGS

Criminal offences broadly fall into two groups: *indictable* offences, which are tried before a judge and jury, and *summary* offences, which are dealt with by Magistrates' Courts. A person may be brought to court in one of three ways:

1 a summons issued by a Justice of the Peace on an 'information' laid by a police officer, official or private citizen;
2 arrest by a police officer authorised by a warrant issued by a Justice of the Peace on a sworn information;
3 arrest without a warrant when the person is 'caught in the act'.

An arrested person must be brought before a Magistrates' Court as quickly as possible. This is because the ancient safeguard of *habeas corpus* is available to prevent unlawful imprisonment or undue delay in bringing a person to trial. A judge may issue a writ of habeas corpus (Latin for 'you must have the body') to require that (the body of) a detained person be brought before a court to enable the lawfulness of the detention to be tested.

In the court room, the magistrate sits on an enclosed dais called the bench. The clerk of court sits at a desk in front of the bench, and the barristers at a table facing it. A witness box, from which evidence is given, is at one side.

The accused person is called the defendant. A defendent charged with a summary offence, will be brought into court, hear the information and charge and be asked to plead 'guilty' or 'not guilty'. If the plea is not guilty, evidence is taken. Each witness called is required to take an oath of affirmation to 'tell the truth, the whole truth and nothing but the truth'. The prosecution is usually conducted by a police officer and the defendant may be represented by a barrister (called counsel). The defendant may give evidence on oath or make an unsworn statement. The magistrate, when both sides have been heard, either convicts and sentences the defendant, or dismisses the case.

It is a fundamental principle of British justice that an accused person is presumed innocent until proved guilty. The prosecution must establish beyond reasonable doubt that a forbidden act was done with criminal intent, by someone old enough to know what they were doing. Ignorance of the law is no excuse, though it may reduce punishment. Presumption of innocence does not apply to some minor statutory offences, such as 'owner-onus' parking breaches, where the defendant has to prove his or her innocence. Also, in many minor offences, it is not necessary to show that the forbidden act was done with criminal intent.

If the defendant is charged with an indictable offence, the Magistrates' Court holds a preliminary inquiry to determine whether the evidence is sufficient to justify trial by the County Court (or equivalent court) or the Supreme Court. The clerk of courts takes a written record of the evidence, called the depositions. The defendant need not offer any defence at this stage. If the magistrate is not satisfied that the defendant has a case to answer, the defendent will be discharged. A defendant committed for trial, will be allowed out on bail or kept in custody until the trial. Some indictable offences may be dealt with summarily by the Magistrates' Court if the defendant consents.

If, at an inquest, the Coroner returns a finding of murder or man-slaughter, the accused person is sent for trial to the Supreme Court without any further preliminary inquiry. The Director of Public Prosecutions (in Victoria) or Attorney-General also has the power to 'present' any person for trial by a judge and jury without a preliminary hearing. In certain circumstances (and only in Victoria), a Grand Jury of twenty-three may be summoned to hold a preliminary inquiry. Such Crown presentments and Grand Jury hearings are very rare.

When a person is committed for trial, the depositions from the lower court are sent to the Director of Public Prosecutions, who prepares the case for prosecution and instructs a Crown Prosecutor to present it in court in the name of the Queen. The accused, as the defendant is now called, is usually represented by a barrister known as the Counsel for the Defence.

Proceedings in the County Court and the Supreme Court are more solemn than in the lower courts. Judges and barristers wear wigs and gowns, Supreme Court judges being clad in full wigs and scarlet gowns. The accused sits in an enclosure called the dock. The charge is read to the accused, who pleads 'guilty' or 'not guilty'. If the plea is 'not guilty', a jury is chosen. Twelve jury members are 'empanelled' from a number of people selected at random by court officials from a jury roll, a list of ordinary citizens liable to be called for jury service. The defence and prosecution may challenge a certain number of the jury as they come forward; they must step down and let others take their place. The jury is sworn in and the case proceeds.

The Crown Prosecutor outlines the case against the accused and calls witnesses, who give their evidence in the form of replies to the prosecutor's questions. This questioning is called examination-in-chief. The defence counsel has the right of cross-examination, that is, of questioning each opposing witness on the evidence given. When the case for the prosecution has been presented, the defence counsel opens the case for the defence, and calls witnesses, who may be cross-examined by the prosecutor. The prosecutor cannot question the accused unless the accused gives evidence on oath or affirmation. An accused who makes an unsworn statement is not subject to cross-examination.

After the counsel for the prosecution and defence have made their final addresses to the jury, the judge sums up the relevant facts and explains points of law. The jury retires to decide whether, on the evidence they have heard, the charge against the accused has been established beyond reasonable doubt. Their verdict must be unanimous. In South Australia, Western Australia (except for crimes punishable by death) and Tasmania, a majority verdict of ten to two is enough to convict.

The court reassembles when the jury has reached its decision. If the verdict is 'not guilty', the accused is free to go. If, in a murder case, it is 'not guilty on the grounds of insanity', the prisoner is ordered to be detained 'during the Governor's pleasure' (until the Governor decides the prisoner can safely be released). If the verdict is 'guilty', the judge passes sentence. The jury has no say in the sentencing, but may recommend mercy. If the jury cannot agree within six hours, it may be discharged and a new trial ordered.

Punishment

The death penalty (by hanging) for such crimes as murder has been abolished under Federal law and in all States except Western Australia, where it has fallen into disuse.

Lesser crimes may be punished by imprisonment or fines, or both. Punishment has several aims: to discourage the offender from repeating the offence, to deter others from doing likewise, and to protect the community by keeping incorrigible offenders in custody. Nowadays, greater efforts are made to encourage offenders to reform, and growing use is made in Victoria of suspended sentences, community service orders, probation and parole. The court may *suspend a sentence* if the convicted person agrees to enter a bond to be of good behaviour for a fixed period. Or, instead of a fine, the magistrate may order that the convicted person perform work of benefit to the community for a period of time. A person may be released on *probation* on specified conditions and under the supervision of probation officers. If the period of probation is completed successfully, the conviction is erased unless the offender is convicted again. *Parole* shortens a gaol sentence to give a prisoner a chance to be rehabilitated in the community under supervision. The court fixes a minimum term of imprisonment the prisoner must serve before being eligible for parole. If the Parole Board decides the prisoner should be paroled, he or she is released, but a prisoner who breaks the conditions of parole, will be returned to gaol to serve the rest of the full term.

CRIMINAL COMPENSATION

Criminal justice has been more concerned with punishing wrongdoers than with compensating their victims. Someone who is injured in a criminal assault may not ordinarily be able to recover damages or compensation if the attacker is not identified or arrested, or has no money. To overcome the problem, Victoria has established a *Crimes Compensation Tribunal* which can award up to $50 000 to compensate victims of violent crimes for pain and suffering, lost earnings and medical expenses.

New South Wales has a criminal compensation scheme under which a judge can order a criminal to pay compensation of up to $10 000. If the criminal cannot pay, the State pays the victim and tries to recover the amount from the criminal later. In some cases, compensation may be paid even if the criminal is not brought to trial.

CIVIL PROCEEDINGS

Civil proceedings in the higher courts are begun by the plaintiff (the person who has a complaint or grievance) obtaining from the court registry a writ of summons against the defendant from whom damages or other remedy is sought. The writ is a document ordering, in the Queen's name, the defendant to 'enter an appearance' within a given time, otherwise judgement may be given in the defendant's absence. If the defendant wants to defend the action, the defendant (or their solicitor) 'enters an appearance', that is, lodges at the court registry a document which indicates that the claim will be contested.

The plaintiff has to set out a precise statement of the claim. To this, the defendant makes a detailed statement of defences. These documents are called 'pleadings'. Further statements and answers may be made until the parties are down to the basic issues they want the court to determine.

The case is now ready for hearing. A judge sitting alone decides questions of both law and fact. If there is a jury, the judge directs it on law and the jury decides the facts. In some cases the jury assesses damages. An important form of remedy is an injunction, which is a court order to prevent the defendant from continuing to do or repeating something injurious to the plaintiff.

Small Claims Tribunals

Growing interest in consumer protection has led the mainland States and the Australian Capital Territory to set up Small Claims Tribunals to settle consumers' grievances quickly and cheaply. In Victoria, the tribunal offers arbitration in disputes between traders and consumers where the claim for payment for goods or services, or relating to an insurance contract, is not more than $3000.

Victoria now also has a separate *Credit Tribunal* to settle disputes between consumers and providers of credit involving amounts of up to $20 000 (except for commercial vehicles and farm machinery, where there is no limit). A *Residential Tenancies Tribunal* deals with disputes between landlords and tenants involving amounts of up to $3000.

Equal opportunity

Some States have established special tribunals to deal with complaints of discrimination. In Victoria, subject to certain exemptions, it is unlawful to discriminate against a person because of his or her status or private life. Status covers sex, marital status, race (including colour, ethnic or national origin), impairment, being a parent, childless or de facto spouse. Private life includes political or religious views. Sexual harassment is also unlawful. Complaints may be made to an Equal Opportunity Commissioner whose officers will try to remedy the matter by conciliation. If this fails, the complaint may be referred to an Equal Opportunities Board for a public hearing.

The Commonwealth has appointed a Human Rights and Equal Opportunity Commission to protect human rights and ensure equality before the law as guaranteed by a number of international treaties to which Australia is a party. The commission consists of a president and commissioners dealing with human rights, race discrimination, sex discrimination and privacy.

The legal profession

The legal profession is traditionally divided into two main classes: barristers and solicitors. Barristers conduct cases in court, and give learned opinions on difficult questions of law. Solicitors attend to the numerous legal problems of their clients. A person who wishes to take legal proceedings consults a solicitor, who will brief a barrister to appear in court.

In New South Wales and Queensland, the two branches of the profession are strictly separate, as in England: a barrister is entitled to practise only as a barrister and a solicitor only as a solicitor. In Victoria all lawyers are entitled by law to practise as both barristers and solicitors, but members of the association of counsellors known as the Victorian Bar are bound by their rules to practise exclusively as barristers. In South Australia, Western Australia, Tasmania and the Federal Territories, lawyers are entitled by law and generally do practise as both barristers and solicitors, although some specialise in court appearance. Separate Bars of those who practise exclusively as barristers have been formed in Perth and Canberra.

Eminent barristers may be appointed Queen's Counsel (QC). This honour entitles them to charge higher fees and formerly required them to appear in court only with a junior counsel (one who is not a QC). The NSW Government has announced its intention to end the use of this title. The NSW Law Institute (representing solicitors) has called for an end to the distinction between barristers and solicitors, but this is being resisted by the NSW Bar.

Judges are chosen by the Government, on the advice of the Attorney-General, from among senior and distinguished barristers, and sometimes solicitors. Their independence from political influence is guaranteed by appointment for life or until they reach a fixed retiring age. Judges of the State intermediate courts have the title 'judge' before their names (Judge Smith) and judges of the High Court, Supreme Courts and higher Federal courts have the title 'Justice' (Justice Smith). Judges in court are addressed as 'Your Honour'; Magistrates and Justices of the Peace as 'Your Worship'.

Industrial arbitration

An unusual feature of Australian government has been the use of compulsory arbitration to settle disputes between employers and employees and to fix wages and working conditions. By the early 1990s, the system was undergoing profound changes, with a move towards collective or enterprise bargaining; that is, direct negotiations and agreements or contracts between trade unions or employees and employers.

Australian arbitration has been compulsory only in the sense that a Federal or State tribunal could order the parties in disputes to appear before it, and after hearing both sides, make an award if an agreement could not be reached by conciliation (helping to reach a settlement by negotiation). Awards or registered agreements are legally binding on the parties. However, strong and militant unions have been able to break awards by going on strike or imposing work bans in spite of arbitration. There has been much controversy over whether penal sanctions should be imposed on unions in these circumstances, or whether unions should be liable to be sued for breach of contract.

Industrial arbitration is complicated in Australia by the existence of two sets of arbitration tribunals, Federal and State. The Federal power of arbitration is limited by the Constitution, the main powers being for 'prevention and settlement of industrial disputes beyond the limits of any one State' and the regulation of Commonwealth public servants. The State tribunals deal only with disputes and conditions within each State. The Federal system has become the more important, as most big trade unions and employers' organisations are organised federally, and formerly set the pace in fixing wages and hours of work.

THE INDUSTRIAL RELATIONS COMMISSION

In 1989 the Industrial Relations Commission replaced the former Australian Conciliation and Arbitration Commission, although its functions and structure are similar. Its future, however, is uncertain. It is likely to continue to settle industrial disputes by conciliation or arbitration. But its traditional role in centralised wage-fixing, either by awards for particular industries or through national wage cases, is being greatly diminished. The Keating Government and the ACTU have agreed that the wages and salaries of most workers should be determined by enterprise or workplace bargaining. Although the Federal Government has no constitutional power to fix wages directly, it may rely on its external affairs power to legislate for a minimum wage, equal pay and redundancy payments to conform with its obligations under international labour treaties.

The Industrial Division of the Federal Court is responsible for enforcing awards made by the Industrial Relations Commission by punishing breaches. It may also inquire into alleged irregularities in trade union elections and to decide points of law referred to it by the commission. There is a limited right of appeal, by its leave, to the High Court.

State industrial or employee relations commissions fix minimum wages, hours of work and conditions of employment for workers who do not come under Federal awards or agreements. In some States, notably Victoria, the trend is also towards enterprise bargaining (with or without unions) and a more limited role for the State tribunal. New South Wales and South Australia also have conciliation committees of employers and union representatives with an independent chairman in many industries to settle disputes.

For further thought

- Is trial by jury an essential safeguard against tyranny or is it no longer warranted in this modern age?
- Should juries assess damages in personal injury cases, or would judges be better qualified to do so?
- Should court cases be heard in public or in private? Give your reasons.
- Who should bear the cost of litigation? Should the loser pay all, or should each party pay their own costs?
- Should there be one arbitration authority in place of the present complex system of Federal and State arbitration bodies of various types?
- Should trade unions be subject to penalties if they order their members to strike?

CHAPTER
13

TERRITORIES

Australia in 1993 had ten Territories, extending from the equator to the South Pole and from the Indian Ocean to the Pacific. On the continent itself are the Northern Territory, the Australian Capital Territory and the Jervis Bay Territory.

The external Territories are: Norfolk Island, the Ashmore and Cartier Islands (deemed part of the Northern Territory), the Cocos (Keeling) Islands, Christmas Island, the Coral Sea Islands Territory, the Heard and McDonald Islands, and the Australian Antarctic Territory.

Three former Australian territories have achieved national independence. Papua and New Guinea became fully self-governing at the end of 1973 and fully independent as a single nation on 16 September 1975. Nauru, a small island in the central Pacific, became fully independent on 31 January 1968. Nauru and New Guinea were German colonies before the First World War. They were entrusted to Australian administration in 1919 under a League of Nations mandate and later as United Nations trust territories. Papua was formerly a British protectorate which came under Australian control in 1905.

The Northern Territory, which might become a State, and the Australian Capital Territory have progressed towards almost full self-government. Norfolk Island, the Cocos Islands and Christmas Island have moved towards more limited self-government. The Minister for Environment, Sport and Territories is responsible for all the Territories.

AUSTRALIAN CAPITAL TERRITORY

In 1988 Australia celebrated the Bicentenary (200th anniversary) of European settlement. One of the main events was the opening by Queen Elizabeth II, on 9 May, of the majestic new Parliament House on Capital Hill in Canberra. It was on the north-eastern slope of this hill on 12 March 1913 that Canberra—the seat of Australia's national capital—was officially born and named.

The surrounding limestone plains, ringed by timber hills and mountains, had been settled and grazed since the 1820s. But by 1913 they had changed little in the century since the Kamberra Branch of the Ngarrugu tribe of Aborigines had held their corroborees there.

That Australia should have a national capital away from the old State capitals had been decided by the fathers of Federation. They wrote into the Constitution that the Commonwealth Parliament should choose its seat of government, but added that it should be in a separate territory of not less than 100 square miles (259 square kilometres), and in New South Wales not less than 100 miles (160 kilometres) from Sydney. As a concession to Victoria, Parliament was to meet in Melbourne until the new capital was established.

Numerous sites for the new territory were considered before an area of about 2330 square kilometres in the Yass–Canberra district was chosen in 1908. After the Federal and New South Wales Parliaments passed the necessary legislation, the area became Commonwealth territory on 1 January 1911.

An international competition was held for the design of the new capital. From 137 designs received, that of a young Chicago architect, Walter Burley Griffin, was chosen. Griffin's plan was grand and inspired. The city was to be laid out in a geometric pattern, based on the natural landmarks, and set in landscaped parkland. The useless flood plain of the Molonglo River was to be a chain of ornamental lakes, with the national buildings, including Parliament House, to the south and the civic and commercial centre to the north.

The First World War interrupted construction of the new city, and it was not until 1927 that Federal Parliament could be transferred from Melbourne to Canberra. On 9 May of that year, the Duke of York (later King George VI) officially opened the 'temporary' Parliament House which remained the seat of Parliament for sixty-one years.

The depression of the 1930s and the Second World War further hindered Canberra's development. Some of the basic principles and proposals of Griffin's plan had been lost. The appointment in 1958 of the National Capital Development Commission marked a turning point. The commission, supported by the Government, blended Griffin's vision with sound planning and development for the needs of a rapidly growing city.

Work began on forming the long-forgotten central lake to unify the halves of the capital. Griffin's parliamentary triangle came into prominence. At the apex of the triangle is Capital Hill, where the foundation stones were laid in 1913. Below Capital Hill, in a direct line to Mount Ainslie, is Parliament House, and beyond the lake the Australian War Memorial. One arm of the triangle extends along Commonwealth Avenue and Bridge to Civic Hall, the focal point of Canberra's civic and commercial centre. Another arm of the triangle is formed by King's Avenue and Bridge and leads to Russell Hill, the site of the Australian–American memorial column and the Defence headquarters. The triangle is completed by Constitution Avenue. The three avenues, King's, Constitution and Commonwealth, are a reminder of the motto of the city's coat of arms: 'For the King, the law and the people'. Within the triangle, on the south-east shore of Lake Burley Griffin, is the new High Court building, opened in May 1980.

From only 6000 residents in 1927 and still only 17 000 in 1947, the population of the Australian Capital Territory has grown to about 300 000. Owing to Canberra's special significance as the national capital, however, the Territory is unlikely ever to become a State. But in 1985 the Federal Government decided that it should have substantial self-government. This was not a popular move among its residents, many of whom feared that they would have to pay more for the administration and services previously provided by Commonwealth authorities. In 1989 a seventeen-member Legislative Assembly replaced the former advisory council, taking over responsibility for most of the services of the kind provided elsewhere by State and local governments.

The first Assembly was elected by the complicated European d'Hondt system of proportional representation, which took about two months to produce the final results. From 1995, members will be elected for three-year terms by the simpler Hare-Clark system similar to that used in Tasmania, with two electorates returning five members each and one returning seven. The Assembly elects a Presiding Officer and Chief Minister, who appoints three other Ministers. In 1992 a Labor Party majority was able to form the ACT Government with the support of Independents.

Since 1974, the Australian Capital Territory elects two members to the House of Representatives and, since 1976, also has two Senators. Until 1966, the member for the Australian Capital Territory could vote only on matters affecting the Territory.

Canberra is no longer just a 'government town'. It is a fast-growing commercial and regional centre and the headquarters and meeting-place for many national organisations. It is a centre of learning and research—the home of the Australian National University, the Academy of Science, Mt Stromlo Observatory, the National Library and important sections of the Commonwealth Scientific and Industrial Research Organisation. Canberra has become a spacious and beautiful national capital of which Australians can feel proud.

JERVIS BAY TERRITORY

As it was thought that the Commonwealth might in future need an area on the coast for a port, an area of about seventy square kilometres at Jervis Bay, 160 kilometres south of Sydney, was reserved in 1915 as part of the Capital Territory. It is now administered separately. Most of the area is used for defence purposes, a nature reserve and Aboriginal land. The 800 residents may vote for Federal elections as part of the electorate of Fraser and for the Senate.

NORTHERN TERRITORY

This huge Territory covers one-sixth of the Australian continent and is almost six times the size of Great Britain. It is 1610 kilometres from north to south and 934 kilometres from east to west. But the population of the Territory is still only about 170 000.

Captain Matthew Flinders explored the coastline in 1803 and Lieutenant Philip King in 1817, but early attempts at settlement failed. In 1825, the area was declared part of New South Wales. A year after the ill-fated expedition of Burke and Wills, John McDouall Stuart completed his crossing of the continent from south to north in 1862. His reports of land suitable for grazing cattle led to the gradual settlement of the Territory and the beginnings of its important pastoral industry.

In July 1863 the Northern Territory became the responsibility of South Australia, and on 1 January 1911 administration of the Territory was transferred to the Commonwealth Government.

In 1978 the Territory became virtually self-governing. Instead of a Governor, there is an Administrator appointed by and responsible to the Commonwealth Government. The former Legislative Council of official and elected members has been replaced by a Legislative Assembly which now has twenty-five members elected for four years. The Territory Government consists of a Chief Minister and eight other Ministers drawn from the majority in the Assembly (in 1985 the Country–Liberal Party).

The Administrator is advised by an Executive Council consisting of the Territory Ministers.

The Legislative Assembly may legislate on all matters affecting the Territory except some 'untransferred' matters such as Aboriginal land rights, uranium mining and national parks. The Northern Territory Government is responsible for the administration of a number of departments and statutory authorities.

Many people in the Territory hope that it will become a State within a few years. The main obstacles are the relatively small population (if the Territory were to have twelve Senators like each of the present States instead of two it would be grossly over represented in Federal Parliament), the heavy financial dependence on the Commonwealth, and the reluctance of the Federal Government to relinquish control over Aboriginal land rights, uranium mining and national parks.

Aboriginal people who are able to prove strong traditional links with unalienated Crown land may make a claim to an Aboriginal Land Commissioner, a judge of the Northern Territory Supreme Court. The Minister for Aboriginal Affairs may accept or reject the commissioner's recommendations. About a third of the Territory's total area has been transferred to Aboriginal freehold tenure.

Local government in the Territory was first established in Darwin in 1957. There are now also five town councils and one shire council. All are elected by adult franchise for four-year terms. In addition, a different form of local government is provided by forty-eight community (mostly Aboriginal) government councils elected for one-year terms. Some are responsible for managing local industries as well as providing community services and amenities.

The Ashmore and Cartier Islands

Situated in the Timor Sea, north-west of Australia, these islands are administered as part of the Northern Territory. They were transferred by Britain to Australia in 1931, and until 1938 were administered by Western Australia.

Norfolk Island

Norfolk Island, discovered by Captain Cook in 1774, lies in the Pacific Ocean, 1610 kilometres north-east of Sydney. It is about eight kilometres long and five kilometres wide. Many of its 2000 inhabitants are descendants of the *Bounty* mutineers from Pitcairn Island.

The island was first settled as early as 1788 by a party led by Lieutenant Philip King from New South Wales, and remained a convict settlement until 1813. In 1825, it was occupied again, and for the next thirty years became notorious as a dreaded punishment station for convicts sent from New South Wales.

In 1856, Norfolk Island became a free and separate settlement as a new home for the whole population of Pitcairn Island, where disease and famine were rife. The Governor of New South Wales was made responsible for administration, and in 1896, the island became a dependency of New South Wales. It was named a Territory of Australia in 1913.

In 1979, the Administrator's former advisory council was replaced by a Legislative Assembly of nine elected members with a wide range of legislative powers. Six of these members have ministerial-type responsibilities and form an Executive Council. Norfolk Island made further progress towards full internal self-government with the transfer of additional powers in 1989. However, the Assembly's real powers are limited by the necessity for the Administrator's assent, which in effect means the Federal Government's consent. The island has its own Supreme Court and Court of Petty Sessions.

COCOS (KEELING) ISLANDS

In the Indian Ocean about half-way between Perth and Sri Lanka lie the Cocos or Keeling Islands, discovered in 1609 by Captain William Keeling of the East India Company. They comprise twenty-seven small coral islands forming two separate atolls. The population of about 650 lives on only two of the islands. The 400 residents of Home Island are of Malay origin while the residents of the larger West Island (about ten kilometres long and half a kilometre wide) are mostly Europeans on short-term government postings.

Two British adventurers, Alexander Hare and John Clunies Ross, established separate settlements on the islands in 1826 and 1827. Hare left after several years, and John Clunies Ross became the first 'King of the Cocos'. Three years after his death, the islands became a British possession in 1857, and John George Clunies Ross was appointed Governor. In 1887, the islands came under the administration of Ceylon (as Sri Lanka was then called) and in 1882 under that of the Straits Settlements (Malaya). In 1903 they became part of the Settlement of Singapore.

Queen Victoria in 1886 granted the islands in perpetuity to the Clunies Ross family, and for sixty years the head of the family was recognised as Resident Magistrate and Government Representative. In 1946, however, the islands became a dependency of Singapore under a Resident Administrator responsible to the Governor of Singapore. The Cocos Islands became an Australian Territory in 1955 by agreement between Britain and Australia.

In 1978, the Australian Government bought for about $6 200 000 most of the territory from its hereditary owner and virtual ruler, John Clunies Ross. The island is administered by an Administrator and a local council elected by the islanders. On 6 April 1984, in an act of self-determination supervised by the United Nations, the Cocos Malay community was given the choice of full independence, 'free association' with Australia, or integration with Australia. The islanders voted for integration. This means that they now are Australian citizens and subject to Australian law. They have full voting rights in Federal elections, being counted as part of the Northern Territory electorate, but also retain direct access to the Minister for Territories. The powers and the responsibilities of the Cocos Islands Council are to be extended.

Christmas Island

Christmas Island is in the Indian Ocean 1450 kilometres from north-west Australia. Australia became responsible for its administration on 1 October 1958. As Nauru did, the island of 142 square kilometres formerly depended entirely on its phosphate deposits. There is no native population. Many of the 1200 remaining residents of Chinese, European and Malay origin are engaged in limited phosphate mining by a private venture and in working in the new casino and holiday resort.

The first recorded landing on the island was by William Dampier in 1688, although it was charted earlier. Captain H.W. May, of *HMS Imperieuse*, annexed the island for Britain in 1888. In the same year, George Clunies Ross, the third 'King of Cocos', settled the island and in 1891 he and Sir John Murray were granted a ninety-nine-year lease. This was transferred to the Christmas Island Phosphate Company in 1897. In 1900 the island came under the administration of Singapore. The Japanese occupied the island from 1942 to 1945.

Christmas Island is now administered by an Administrator responsible to the Minister for Environment, Sport and Territories. Since 1885 there has been a Christmas Island Assembly of nine members elected by proportional representation for one-year terms. It directs the Christmas

Island Services Corporation, which provides local and community services. Residents who are Australian citizens may also vote in Federal elections, being enrolled for the Northern Territory.

CORAL SEA ISLANDS

Scattered over 1 036 000 square kilometres east of Queensland, these tiny, low-lying islands and reefs became Australia's newest territory in September 1969. None of the islands, which are little more than sand-banks, has any permanent inhabitants, but one, Willis Island, has had a manned weather station since 1921.

AUSTRALIAN ANTARCTIC TERRITORY

Almost half of the vast icy Antarctic continent is Australian territory. Although not all nations recognise Australia's territorial claim, Australian exploration and scientific research in the Antarctic has won world-wide acclaim. The Territory, cut into two by a narrow sector of French terri-tory (Adélie Land), has an area of 6 216 000 square kilometres, about four-fifths the size of Australia.

What is now Australian Antarctic Territory was first sighted by a British sealer in 1831. The huge white continent captured the imagination of adventurous men of several nations, and Britain, France and the United States sent expeditions to the Antarctic in 1840. It was not until the Australasian Antarctic expedition led by Douglas Mawson (1912–13) that men wintered there on land.

In 1929–31, Mawson led a British–Australian–New Zealand expedi-tion to the Antarctic with authority to take possession of lands already discovered by British explorers and to hoist the flag on newly found land. In 1933, Britain placed a large sector of the polar continent under the authority of the Commonwealth of Australia.

The first permanent Australian Antarctic research stations were set up at Heard Island and Macquarie Island by the Australian National Antarctic Research Expeditions (ANARE) in the summer of 1947–48. An Antarctic Division was created in the External Affairs Department in 1949 to administer the expeditions. In 1968, responsibility for the Antarctic Division was transferred to the Minister for Supply, and in 1972 to the Minister for Science.

In 1954 the ANARE established a station on the coast of MacRobertson Land and named it Mawson. In 1955 the Heard Island station was closed down, but in 1957 another station, Davis, was established on the Antarctic mainland, this time on the coast of Princess Elizabeth Land, 640 kilometres east of Mawson. In 1959, Australia took over an American base, Wilkes, set up during the International Geophysical Year (1957–58). This was replaced in 1969 by a new station, Casey, about two and a half kilometres south of Wilkes.

Australia's four permanent Antarctic stations—Mawson, Davis, Casey and Macquarie Island—have become important centres for scientific research in many fields, for sources of weather forecasting information and for further exploration. Each year teams of scientists set forth by ice-breaker to spend twelve months at these lonely outposts until they are replaced by relief teams.

Under an international protocol involving twenty-six nations with territorial or scientific interests in Antarctica, the continent and continental shelf have been declared a natural reserve devoted to peace and science. Mining is banned.

HEARD ISLAND AND THE MCDONALD ISLANDS

Heard Island and the McDonald Islands were transferred by Britain to Australia in 1947. Heard Island, 4025 kilometres south-west of Perth, is about forty-four kilometres long and twenty-one kilometres wide. The small, steep and rocky McDonald Islands are forty-two kilometres west of Heard Island. Macquarie Island is regarded as a dependency of Tasmania.

For further thought

- Many people in the Australian Capital Territory were not keen on internal self-government. What were the arguments for and against making residents financially and otherwise responsible for services provided elsewhere by State governments or local authorities?
- Should the Northern Territory become Australia's seventh State? Why or why not?
- What is the value of manning research stations in the Antarctic? Should mining be allowed if valuable mineral deposits are found there?
- What form of self-government should be granted to Australia's inhabited island Territories?

14

AUSTRALIA AND THE WORLD

From a dumping ground for convicts in a remote corner of the British Empire, Australia has grown to be a fully independent and self-governing nation, free to speak and act in world affairs. By European standards, we are a young nation. But measured against the sudden bursting into independence of former colonies in Africa and Asia in recent years, our growth to nationhood was a gradual one.

GROWTH TO NATIONHOOD

A rebellion in Canada in 1837 began a constitutional evolution that is still going on in parts of the British Commonwealth today. In his famous report of 1839 on the political discontent in Canada, Lord Durham recommended a system of responsible self-government. The Governor should act in local affairs on the advice of his colonial Ministers, who should be chosen from and responsible to the fully elected legislature. Once introduced in Canada, responsible government spread to the Australian colonies in 1856 and later to New Zealand and South Africa.

However, the powers of the colonial governments were still limited. Britain kept control over foreign relations, trade and disposal of Crown lands, and she could make laws for the colonies. The colonies could not amend their own constitutions or make laws 'repugnant' (contrary) to any British law applying within their boundaries. The Governors could still refuse assent to any Bill. Even if assent were given, legislation could be disallowed by the British Government. The Governors were also entitled, and in some cases required, to reserve for Royal Assent any Bill passed by the colonial parliaments.

It took nearly a century after the Durham Report for all these limitations to be removed. Many ceased to apply in fact before they were abolished in law as the colonies pressed for greater freedom. By the late 1850s the colonies gained control over lands and to a large extent over tariffs. Later, they were allowed to enter into foreign trade agreements.

Federation in 1901 gave Australia a national Government that—within the framework of the Constitution—speaks and acts for the country as a whole. The Commonwealth Constitution, unlike Canada's, was essentially drawn up by Australians for Australians in the 1890s. After approval by the Australian people in two sets of referendums, it was passed by the British Parliament with only minor alterations relating to appeals to the Privy Council. The Federal Parliament was given powers over external affairs (though it did not use these fully for some time), defence, trade and immigration. The Federal Constitution could be amended by referendum without the consent of the British Parliament.

At an Imperial Conference in 1907, the term *dominion* was adopted to describe the self-governing members of the Empire outside Britain. The British Government gradually withdrew its control over the Dominion parliaments. A Governor-General rarely refused assent to legislation, and Bills were seldom disallowed except in a few cases where they affected British interests or went beyond the powers of Parliament.

The *Imperial Conference of 1926* defined the Dominions as:

> autonomous communities within the British Empire, equal in status, in no way subordinate one to another in any aspect of their domestic or external affairs, though united by a common allegiance to the Crown and freely associated as members of the British Commonwealth of Nations.

The Conference also declared what already had become fact—that:

> the Governor-General of a Dominion is the representative of the Crown holding in all essential respects the same position in relation to the administration of public affairs in a Dominion as is held by His Majesty the King in Great Britain.

The Governor-General was no longer to be the representative of the British Government as well as of the Sovereign.

The *Imperial Conference of 1930* agreed that the Governor-General should be appointed on the advice of the Dominion's Ministers and not on that of British Ministers. This conference also placed on record that the power of the British Government to disallow or reserve legislation no longer operated.

The *Statute of Westminster* (1931) gave legal form to some of the resolutions of the 1926 and 1930 conferences. No British Act of Parliament was in future to apply to any Dominion except by its request or with its consent. Each Dominion was given power to make laws that applied beyond its boundaries (for example, over shipping). The Dominions could repeal or amend any British Act that formed part of their law (but not the Australian Constitution). No Dominion law was to be invalid because it was 'repugnant' to any British law.

The Statute of Westminster did not apply to Australia until it had been adopted by the Australian Parliament. Strangely, this did not happen until 1942, when it became necessary to enable the Australian Government to extend wartime control over shipping. The Statute did not apply to the Australian States, but the British Government was no longer interested in interfering in their affairs.

In 1949 the concept of Australian citizenship was introduced. Previously, Australians were British subjects who happened to be born (or naturalised) in Australia. A few years later, Australians ceased to be British subjects as well as Australian citizens.

The *Australia Act 1986* relieved the Queen of any real executive powers (which she had long ceased to exercise, anyway) over the Australian Commonwealth and States. This legislation also severed such remaining relics as legal appeals to the Privy Council, the dormant right of the British Parliament to legislate for Australia, and the application of some old imperial statutes in the Australian States.

INTERNATIONAL RELATIONS

Before 1914, Australia and the other Dominions had no decisive say in international affairs. Britain agreed to consult the Dominions where their interests were at stake, but made it clear that she alone controlled Imperial foreign policy. As early as the 1870s and 1880s, the Australian colonies had expressed fears about German and French activities in the Pacific, and largely as the result of Australian agitation Britain annexed Fiji in 1874 and made British New Guinea (Papua) a protectorate in 1884. Nationalist feelings and a determination to have some control over our defence led to the beginnings of the Royal Australian Navy in 1907 and the establishment of the Royal Military College, Duntroon, in 1911. Isolated by distance and protected by the might of the British Navy, Australia was, however, more concerned with affairs at home.

The First World War plunged Australia into new responsibilities of nationhood. The heroism of the Anzacs at Gallipoli and the courage and endurance of the first AIF in France and the Middle East brought Australia a new stature in the eyes of Britain and the rest of the world. Australia and the other Dominions were given a place in the British War Cabinet in 1917 and 1918, attended the peace conference as separate signatories, and became original members of the League of Nations.

It was not until the Second World War, however, that Australia adopted a foreign policy of its own. With the loss of Singapore, Malaysia and the Dutch East Indies to the Japanese in 1941–42, Australia realised that Britain could no longer guarantee security. For the first time, Australia faced the threat of invasion. Late in 1941, the Prime Minister, Mr John Curtin, made his famous direct appeal to the United States to come to our aid. The Americans responded and, under General Douglas MacArthur, supported by Australian forces, turned back the enemy.

After the war, the world situation had changed. The British Navy no longer ruled the waves. The United States and Soviet Russia emerged as the dominant powers. In an effort to safeguard future generations against the scourge of war, the nations of the world formed the United Nations. But much of the world was soon drawn into a 'cold war' between America and Russia and their allies.

In our part of the world, one after another of the former British and European colonies in Asia won independence. India, Pakistan and Ceylon became independent members of the Commonwealth of Nations; the Dutch East Indies emerged as Indonesia; and in French Indo-China there was a bitter struggle and division into the independent States of Vietnam, Laos and Cambodia. Mainland China came under Communist control and in Western eyes replaced Japan as the main potential threat to peace and stability in East Asia.

From 1949 to 1971, American—and Australian—policy sought to 'contain' China and help countries in the region resist aggression and subversion. In 1950 Australia was one of fifteen United Nations members to send troops to Korea to repel Communist invaders from the north. In the 1960s, Australia, in partnership with the United States and other allies, became deeply involved in the war in Vietnam, in support of the anti-Communist government in Saigon in the south against Communist forces led from Hanoi in the north.

By the early 1970s the world situation had changed again. The United States had reached an understanding with the Soviet Union in an effort to replace the 'cold war' with peaceful co-existence. The Soviet Union and Communist China had become increasingly hostile towards each other. America, unable to accomplish its aims in Vietnam and under growing pressure at home and abroad to withdraw its forces from Vietnam, and China, concerned about possible conflict with the Soviet Union, decided to improve their mutual relations. Australia also withdrew its troops from

Vietnam and established diplomatic relations with China. Meanwhile, Britain joined the European Economic Community and British influence 'east of Suez' declined. Japan emerged as an economic super-power, increasingly independent of America.

By the early 1990s, further dramatic changes had occurred. Communist rule collapsed in Russia and Eastern Europe, and the once monolithic Soviet Union disintegrated into its component republics, loosely allied under the title of Commonwealth of Independent States. The 'cold war' had ended, and with it, fears of a possible nuclear war between the superpowers, although tensions remained in the Middle East and other local trouble spots.

The world is no longer split simply into two major groupings, one led by the United States and the other by the Soviet Union. China, Japan and Western Europe have grown in importance, and smaller nations, such as Australia, are striving for a more independent outlook.

AUSTRALIAN FOREIGN POLICY

The foreign policy of any nation is directed towards preserving and furthering certain basic national interests. Australia has traditionally had four main national interests. They have been generally supported by all major political parties and most people, although the emphasis has altered over time with changing circumstances, and not everyone has agreed on how best to uphold them. The first interest is to maintain national security through international diplomacy and a readiness to defend the continent and territories against possible armed attack or other aggression. The second is to protect and promote the nation's economic welfare and living standards, which increasingly depend on global economic growth, unhindered international trade and the confidence of global financial markets. The third is to keep our democratic way of life, and our civil and political liberties. The fourth, and this is more controversial and might be less enduring, has been to preserve our basic communal character.

Australia, for reasons both of international morality and national self-interest, also tries to be a cooperative neighbour in its region and a conscientious member of the world community. This includes a concern for human rights, willingness to resettle refugees, opposition to racism, efforts to reduce environmental pollution and preserve the natural heritage, and support for disarmament and peace-keeping missions. Sometimes these objectives conflict: for instance, when Australia feels obliged to protest against human rights violations in countries with which it also wishes to maintain defence or trade links.

Australia is a large country with a small population and limited power. Our history has made us a nation of largely European origin, culture and thought, but our geography binds us to Asia and the Pacific. Australian foreign policy reflects both our history and our geography. We aim to protect and advance Australian interests, remembering that our welfare and security are bound up with those of others. For this reason, we work for a world order based on the principles and purposes of the United Nations, of which we were a founding member. Our policies are increasingly shaped by our direct and special interest in the countries of Asia and the Pacific. This is expressed through diplomatic missions and in regional cooperation. We also recognise that our relations with countries of the Commonwealth are of a special kind. We remain allied with the United States to reinforce our security, but no longer feel so closely bound to American policies. We recognise that Japan is vital to us as a trading partner, and that China is developing as a major economic power.

Defence, trade and immigration policies are closely bound up with foreign policy. The importance of *trade policy* is indicated by the merger of Foreign Affairs and Trade into a single department and the growing emphasis on trade relations by our diplomatic missions abroad. This recognises the growing interdependence of the world economy. The core of the trade policy is to protect and expand our export markets, to maintain stable prices for our commodities, and to press for free access for our agricultural, mineral and manufactured products. Australia is a strong supporter of efforts through the General Agreement on Tariffs and Trade (GATT) to liberalise world trade and counter protectionist tendencies, and initiated the fourteen-member Cairns Group of Fair Traders in Agriculture. Australia also launched the Asia–Pacific Economic Cooperation (APEC) grouping to foster regional economic relations and trade. This forum includes the ASEAN nations (Indonesia, Malaysia, Philippines, Thailand, Singapore and Brunei), Japan, South Korea, China, Taiwan, Hong Kong, the United States, Canada and New Zealand. Australia has a Closer Economic Relations (CER) agreement with New Zealand for the free movement of goods between the two countries.

Australia's *immigration policy* since the Second World War has gone through two main phases. In the 1950s and 1960s, it was directed towards national development through population growth, while maintaining a predominantly homogenous population. Australia offered plenty of jobs and good living conditions, and many immigrants were attracted by an assisted migration scheme which provided passages for the payment of only $20 a person. The huge influx of immigrants has boosted Australia's population by more than three million permanent settlers since 1945 and led to rapid economic growth. It also enriched Australia's social and cultural life. The restrictive side of the policy limited the entry of persons not of British or other European descent, with the aim of enabling Australia to remain essentially free of the racial and social problems that have troubled some other countries.

In the 1970s and 1980s, both the positive and negative aspects of the immigration policy were modified. With the onset of economic recession and growing unemployment, the immigration intake was reduced and generally limited to refugees, family members of immigrants already here, and skilled workers for whom there was still a demand. The emphasis thus shifted from economic to social and humanitarian objectives. At the same time, the policy no longer excluded immigrants on grounds of racial origin, colour of skin or nationality. The current policy may be said to be selective, but not discriminatory.

In the early 1990s, the severe economic recession and prospect of continuing high unemployment led to a further reduction in the total immigration intake and a debate over selection of immigrants to be admitted. Some experts argue that immigration boosts economic growth by creating extra demand for goods and services and therefore jobs. Others say that immigrants, especially those with few skills and from non-English-speaking countries, find it difficult to get jobs and fit in, and put a heavy strain on social services. Some people oppose mass immigration of any kind on environmental grounds.

REPRESENTATION ABROAD

Australia had no direct diplomatic representatives overseas before the Second World War except in London. In 1940, Mr R.G. (later Lord) Casey went to Washington as Australian Minister to open our first diplomatic mission in a foreign country. This was soon followed by missions to Japan, China and Canada. Today Australia has diplomatic, trade and consular representatives based in more than seventy countries, some accredited to more than one country in a particular region. Some

AUSTRALIA'S BEST COASTAL DEFENCE

missions also include immigration officials. We also have missions to the United Nations and some other international organisations. About seventy foreign and Commonwealth countries have missions here.

DEFENCE POLICY

The basic aims of our defence policy are to safeguard our shores and territories against armed aggression, to keep our trade routes and communications open and to protect our national interests. These include a concern for peace and stability in our regional neighbourhood. In recent years, Australia has increasingly taken part in United Nations peace-keeping operations in trouble spots of strategic interest to this country.

In theory, several defence options are open to Australia. Some people believe we should follow a policy of disarmament and neutrality, or non-alignment with any of the great powers, reliance on the United Nations to settle international disputes, friendship with our neighbours, and limited 'police-type' armed forces. But most Australians would not accept the risk of such a policy in an uncertain and imperfect world.

Others argue for what has been called a 'fortress Australia' policy, relying on strong, home-based armed forces, possibly equipped with nuclear weapons, rather than on great power alliances and regional involvement. This proposal assumes that we cannot really rely on others to defend us, but can make it hard for anyone to attack us. It would mean, however, much bigger spending on defence, leaving less money available for development and other needs.

A third option, which Australia followed since the Second World War until recently, is to take sides and become actively involved in regional security. Our defence policy in this period rested on military alliances and cooperation, principally with the United States through the ANZUS Treaty and the South-East Asia Collective Defence Treaty (SEATO), and on defence arrangements with Britain, New Zealand, Malaysia and Singapore. As contributions to a 'forward defence' policy, we joined the United States and others in trying to stop Communist expansion in South-East Asia (for instance, by sending troops to Vietnam) and, with Britain and New Zealand, in helping Malaysia and Singapore resist insurgency and build up their defence capacity.

At the beginning of the 1970s, changes in the emphasis of our defence policy emerged. The United States, without withdrawing from its treaty obligations, called on its friends and allies to take a greater responsibility for their own security, both individually and collectively. This 'Nixon doctrine', followed by the American withdrawal from Vietnam and accompanied by the decline in British power and influence east of Suez, means that Australia will have to become more self-reliant in defence and less a supporter of the commitments of great powers and more a partner with other countries in its region.

Since 1972, Australian Governments have been developing a new defence policy which draws on elements of all three options mentioned. The ANZUS Treaty is a defence pact between Australia, New Zealand and the United States, signed in 1951 with the original intention of safeguarding the region against any re-emergence of militarism by Japan. Then its focus switched to the possibility of Communist aggression. With the end of the Cold War and establishment of diplomatic and trade relations with China, the importance of ANZUS has faded.

The SEATO partners in 1975 decided to phase out their 21-year-old alliance, formed to counter Soviet, Chinese or other Communist expansion in South-East Asia and invoked to justify American and Australian intervention in Vietnam. However, Australia's alliance with the United States, including joint defence facilities in this country, remains a cornerstone of defence policy. It is understood, though, that the US would not necessarily respond to every perceived threat to Australia in the region.

As its defence advisers could foresee no major threat to Australian security for the next fifteen years, the Whitlam Government decided to end compulsory military service, to reduce the size of our defence forces, and to support moves for a lessening of tension and great power rivalry in the region. The following Liberal–NCP Government decided in 1976 that the 'no-threat-for-fifteen-years' forecast was too optimistic in an unstable world and that Australia's defence capability should be strengthened. It declared that the nation should be prepared to meet such contingencies as: guerrilla or terrorist violence; friction arising from disputes over territorial waters, fishing rights, air space or access to offshore mineral, oil and gas deposits; pressures resulting from competition between the superpowers (especially Russia) for influence in the Indian Ocean; and a decline or shift in the global situation.

The Hawke and Keating Labor Governments have continued their commitment to a self-reliant defence policy, while maintaining the American alliance, fostering cooperation with regional neighbours and pressing for international disarmament. An important defence policy statement in 1987 announced a major re-equipment of the Australian Defence Force to give the concept of self-defence more teeth. Since then, Australia has increasingly contributed to international peacekeeping operations, such as in Cambodia and Somalia, and took part in the 1990 Gulf War against Iraq. Some critics believe that our defence forces have become stretched too thinly to respond adequately to any emergency nearer home.

THE COMMONWEALTH OF NATIONS

The British Empire, since the Second World War, has been transformed into the Commonwealth—a free association of independent and self-governing nations, together with their territories. From eight countries in 1950, Commonwealth membership rose to eleven in 1960, thirty in 1970, and fifty independent members, plus their territories, in 1993. Several territories formerly under British rule or mandate did not join the Commonwealth. Three nations—Ireland, South Africa and Pakistan—left the Commonwealth, but Pakistan rejoined in 1989. Fiji's membership lapsed after a military coup in 1987.

Twenty-nine members of the Commonwealth are republics, sixteen are realms that recognise Queen Elizabeth II as their Head of State, and five (Malaysia, Brunei, Lesotho, Swaziland and Tonga) have their own monarchs. However, all Commonwealth countries acknowledge the Queen as 'the symbol of the free association of the independent member nations and as such Head of the Commonwealth'.

As a family of nations, the Commonwealth is unique. It covers about a quarter of the world's land surface and about a quarter of the world's population. The member nations vary widely in size, history, race, language, culture, religion, development and world importance. All but one were once dependent on Britain, but having 'grown up', they have freely chosen to remain associated with Britain and each other. Their relationship does not rest on a written constitution or hard and fast rules, but on goodwill, sentiment and a varying degree of community of interest. The bonds that hold Commonwealth countries together are thinner than they were, but they still exist.

Commonwealth Governments consult each other on matters of common interest and cooperate in many ways. Commonwealth heads of government meet every two years. There may also be regional meetings, and occasional meetings of Ministers and officials involved in such subjects as finance, defence, education, law and health. Such meetings, and the exchange of information and views, are arranged through the small Commonwealth Secretariat set up at Marlborough House, London, in 1965. Commonwealth Games are held every four years. Commonwealth Governments are represented in each other's capitals by High Commissioners.

THE UNITED NATIONS

Australia is a foundation member of the United Nations. The fifty nations which met in San Francisco in 1945 to draft and adopt the United Nations Charter have been joined by about 130 others. The Charter is the 'constitution' of the organisation, containing its aims and purposes and rules. New members are admitted if they are 'peace-loving' and agree with the aims and to the rules of the Charter, and are accepted by the General Assembly on the recommendation of the Security Council.

The United Nations has six main organs: the General Assembly, Security Council, International Court of Justice, Economic and Social Council, Trusteeship Council and Secretariat. Linked with these are numerous specialised agencies, commissions and committees.

The *General Assembly* is the great forum of world opinion, where all members are represented equally. The Assembly can discuss and make recommendations on any matter mentioned in the Charter. Each nation has one vote, and important questions are decided by a two-thirds majority. The Assembly meets every year at the United Nations permanent headquarters in New York. In 1948 the General Assembly adopted a Declaration of Human Rights.

The *Security Council* is responsible for keeping international peace and security. It may look into any dispute or threat to peace brought to its notice. If necessary, it may authorise the use of armed force to restore order, as it did in Korea and the Congo. The Council has fifteen members. The 'Big Five' World War II allies—Britain, the United States, the Soviet Union, France and China—are permanent members. Ten non-permanent members are elected every two years by the General Assembly. A resolution must be carried by at least nine of the fifteen members, including the 'Big Five', any one of which can veto the resolution by voting 'no'.

The *International Court of Justice* consists of fifteen judges elected by the General Assembly and Security Council for nine-year terms. It considers legal disputes brought before it by nations, such as questions of international law or interpretation of treaties, and gives legal advice to other United Nations bodies. Decisions are by majority vote. The court sits at The Hague.

The *Economic and Social Council*, through its regional and functional commissions and its specialised agencies, works for better social, economic, education and health conditions throughout the world, and for a respect for human rights and freedoms. It consists of fifty-four members elected for three years by the General Assembly. The specialised agencies include the United Nations Educational, Scientific and Cultural Organisation (UNESCO), Food and Agricultural Organisation (FAO), World Health Organisation (WHO), International Labour Organisation (ILO) and International Bank for Reconstruction and Development. There are five regional commissions, including the Economic and Social Commission for Asia and the Pacific (ESCAP), of which Australia is a member.

The *Trusteeship Council* was set up to supervise the administration by member countries of UN Trust Territories. All but one of the eleven original Trust Territories have achieved independence or joined independent countries. The exception, administered by the United States, is the Republic of Belau (Palau), a group of islands in the Western Pacific.

The *Secretariat* provides the routine administration of the United Nations. Its head is the *Secretary-General*.

Australia has played a prominent role in the United Nations and its agencies since it was founded, and has consistently supported it principles and objectives. An Australian, Dr H.V. Evatt, was elected President of the General Assembly in 1948, a tribute for his fight for the rights of small nations. The United Nations has not always succeeded in preserving peace, mainly because it cannot effectively intervene unless the great powers in the Security Council or a majority of nations in the General Assembly agree. For this reason, Australia and other countries have placed great importance on regional defence alliances made in accordance with United Nations principles. The most successful and valuable work of the United Nations is done by its various agencies to raise the living standards, health and education of the poor, sick and hungry millions of the world's population.

For further thought

- To what extent can a medium-sized nation such as Australia maintain an independent foreign policy?
- Should Australia be prepared to fight beyond its shores, with or without allies, or should our defence policy be directed towards defence of the continent?
- What are the benefits and drawbacks of joint US–Australian defence facilities in Australia?
- In what circumstances, if any, would compulsory military training and service be justified?
- What role can the Commonwealth of Nations play? Can it survive as an association of countries with various forms of government and divergent interests?

INDEX